Nudged by the Spirit

Stories of People Responding
to the Still, Small Voice of God

Charlotte Fardelmann

Nudged by the Spirit

Stories of People Responding to the Still, Small Voice of God

by
Charlotte Lyman Fardelmann

Pendle Hill Publications
Wallingford, Pennsylvania 19086

For information please address Pendle Hill Publications
338 Plush Mill Road,
Wallingford, Pennsylvania 19086-6099
1-800-742-5150

All photographs in this book (except where noted)
are by the author, Charlotte Lyman Fardelmann.
Cover photo and leaf photograph on back cover by
Charlotte Lyman Fardelmann
Photograph of author on back cover by
Memories Studio, Rye, New York

Printed in the United States of America by
Thomson-Shore, Inc., Dexter, Michigan

Library of Congress Cataloging-in-Publication Data

Fardelmann, Charlotte Lyman, 1928-
    Nudged by the Spirit: stories of people responding to the
    still, small voice of God/ by Charlotte Lyman Fardelmann.
        p. cm.
    ISBN 0-87574-938-0
    1. Spiritual life--Society of Friends. 2. Christian life--Quaker
    authors. I. Title

BX7738 .F37 2001
289.6'092'2--dc21
[B]   2001037344

To my Children—*Shelley, Mary, George, and James*

Grandchildren—*Galen, Karen, Chelsea, and Haley*

and
Step grand- children—*Bo and Lilia*

TABLE OF CONTENTS

Foreword

Many members of the Religious Society of Friends claim "that of God in everyone" as the foundation for their faith and of their social witness for peace and justice. I'd like to explore the assumptions that give body to this beloved phrase. These assumptions are rarely articulated, and in fact, individuals who consider themselves Friends may vehemently disagree with one or more of them. I share them as my understanding of the fundamental basis for our way of worship, for doing the business of the meeting, for social action, and for being "nudged by the Spirit" in the way the stories in this book illustrate.

Since so many Friends unite in believing there is "that of God" in everyone, the first and critical assumption is that God is. The great "I AM" exists, is real. In one of the Bible's oldest stories, Moses encountering God in the burning bush, God introduces God's self to humans by way of the statement of divine existence: "I am that I am." In spite of the efforts of St. Thomas Aquinas and the Scholastics and philosophers, I do not believe that one can arrive at a very satisfactory understanding of God's existence through reason alone. Through the millennia humans have known this fact: God is. For 350 years Friends have experienced its reality.

The second assumption is that this God who exists loves us—loves all of us and each of us. Both testaments of the Bible tell stories of divine love reaching out to bring us back into right relation with God. Friends' stories abound with examples of responding to threatening situations with love because the Friend had already experienced God's overwhelming love and could move with confidence from that inward place of peace and security.

This brings us to the third assumption: that this God who loves us cares what we do. Both individually and corporately what choices we make matter to God and matter to the whole of creation. Early Friends spoke of the great human and cosmic struggle for and against God's way as the Lamb's War. Even small acts of faithfulness make a difference in the great scheme of things. Both as individuals and as a faith community our choice of actions is vitally important.

The fourth assumption is that since what we choose makes a difference, this God who loves us, communicates with us. God instructs, guides, and teaches us. Early Friends understood that God sent Jesus of Nazareth and the universal Spirit of Christ into the world to teach and lead us.

The fifth assumption is that we can apprehend God's instructions and guidance. If God spoke and we were unable to hear, what would be the point? It is possible for us, both as individuals and as a gathered body, to comprehend God's loving guidance. It does not require a priest, a book, or any intermediary. Without creed, liturgy, or hierarchy, early Friends developed a structure and a process to support listening for divine guidance, and for testing—discerning—what is heard. We have not always followed God's leadings well; today we sometimes feel that we have forgotten much of what Friends once understood and practiced. But the Holy Spirit has not abandoned us. The Inward Teacher is still at work among us, patiently encouraging us to listen, to learn, to bring increasing parts of our individual and corporate life into congruence with pure Love.

In this super-individualistic age it is helpful to see that the main characters in each of the following stories turned to a faith community for help. The "lone Quaker" is an oxymoron. We are a Religious Society, a gathered people, who in community help each other listen, learn, and follow divine guidance. Our meetings provide encouragement and support. They supply warnings and admonitions when we need them. And, because we are all human, our meetings also provide the laboratory in which we inevitably hurt each other and can also heal, forgive, and learn to live together within God's enfolding love.

The stories Charlotte Fardelmann has collected here are heuristic; they demonstrate how leadings happen, and they encourage us to investigate further. They show not only how the Spirit is working, but what she is actively teaching us today. A renewed interest flourishes among Friends in ministry and its symbiotic partnership with eldering/mentoring. Our meetings for worship and for business strive to understand and support what God is bringing forth among us, and the individuals through whom it is coming. The same Teacher who taught early Friends, and before them, the early Christians, is trying to call us forth. We are being taught how to discern which instructions are divine and which are not, how to support and nurture ministry, and how to respond when God touches and transforms our lives—or the life of a member of our meeting—and everything is changed. Because we do this discernment without priests and liturgy, we must pay close attention to the nuances of how the Spirit moves.

Each of the stories in this volume exemplifies not a stage or step, but a characteristic of hearing and responding to God's guidance. Charlotte focuses on a specific nuance of a leading in her introduction to each piece. Her well-chosen quotations anchor each story in a wider experience. These individuals are not unique in their hearing, any more than is the Religious Society of Friends. Throughout time and across cultures the universal Christ, the Word, is available to teach and guide anyone and everyone who humbly listens.

These stories remind us of the wholeness of the full Quaker experience. Quaker faith and practice has been described as a three-legged stool. The legs are the inner, personal relationship with God and the spiritual disciplines that support an interior life; corporate life in a meeting community that worships, works, hurts and heals together; and social testimonies acted out in the wider world that speak of what we are learning inwardly and together. Some Friends are drawn more strongly to one leg than another, and at different times in our lives one leg may predominate over another. But if any leg is completely ignored or cut off, the stool will topple. All three legs are needed both by individual Friends and by each meeting for worship and for business.

The seasons of life flow in their rhythm; ultimately, how God works is a mystery. These stories are teaching tools to help us better understand the ways "the Lord deals with" us. They expand our understanding of the possibilities that may open to us. They point to the support we can offer to others who are being touched and led by the Spirit as we all seek to live the mystery of God's unconditional love for every human being. They help Friends and others know how to respect and respond to "that of God" in everyone.

—Martha Paxson Grundy
Quaker Historian

Preface and Acknowledgements

And Behold, the Lord passed by, and a great strong wind
rent the mountains, and brake in pieces the rocks before
the Lord; but the Lord was not in the wind: and after the
wind an earthquake but the Lord was not in the earth-
quake: And after the earthquake a fire; but the Lord was
not in the fire; and after the fire a still small voice.

I Kings 19:11-12 (KJV)

I was nudged by the Spirit to write this book. It is a book of stories about people of today who, like Elijah, have listened to God and are heeding the promptings of that voice. These people are creating positive changes in the world: teaching, healing, farming, working for peace and justice, writing books, helping others through the creative arts, advocating for the oppressed, working with prisoners, going on pilgrimage, praying for others, working in philanthropic enterprise, and developing ecumenical relationships.

These people are not saints. They are people who were nudged by the Spirit and have responded to the best of their ability. Readers seeking to follow their own divine leadings may be encouraged by the way the Spirit guides and nurtures these people through their struggles. All but one of the people whose stories are told are Quakers, members of the Religious Society of Friends. While many of the stories relate to traditional areas of Quaker service—peace activism, prison work, or education—other types of service have been in-

xiii

cluded to indicate the wide range of God's work in the world. Two of the Quakers in this book have strong Jewish roots as well. A Buddhist peace activist who leads pilgrimages to awaken awareness of the nuclear threat is included. Since spiritual journey is a universal experience, not limited to any one religion, it is my hope that this book will speak truth which can be heard by spiritual seekers.

Responding to God is a creative process. I have known this process at work in my own story told in chapter I. I was nudged by the Spirit to create a charitable fund to support Friends and others by offering financial support and prayer. In my work as administrator of the Lyman Fund, board members and I support those who feel led to take a certain step which leads to more steps and to service in the world. Regular gatherings for grant recipients have become a rich time of story telling. Grantees tell each other about how it has been for them as they followed their leadings, rejoicing, despairing, struggling to do what they felt they must do. They illustrate how each one of us can become co-creators with God in forming the great tapestry of spiritually-based work in the world. From them, I have been confirmed in my understanding of God's creative work in us.

I see this process as a four-stage cycle: input, gestation, creation, and completion. The first stage is a time of "input" when something happens in our lives which disturbs our equilibrium, inflicts us with a concern, and brings out our compassion. Into such a condition God speaks through the "still, small voice"—the voice we may be able to hear when we center down and quiet our minds. This is the voice of Truth and Love within us. The next stage is one of "gestation," mulling it over, praying for guidance, waiting, and seeking clarity about what action to take.

While these first two stages are primarily inward, the next two stages turn us outward. In stage three, "creation," a decision is made, a step taken—to write a few pages, to propose a workshop, to go on pilgrimage, or to take a sabbatical leave. The fourth stage comes at the time when one's creation is offered up to the world. I call this stage "going public." At this point the creation takes on a life of its own as it goes out into the world. The book is published, the workshop takes place, the pilgrimage is going on, a new direction for life is discovered. The creative process has come full circle.

Completing the circle does not mean the cycle is over. Feedback becomes a springboard for input into the next round of the cycle. The path of creative process is not a closed circle but rather a spiral.

Writing this book has followed the stages of creative process. These stories nudged me, inspired me, and required of me that I write them.

This book includes fourteen stories. Each person interviewed has given permission to publish his or her story. These people have taught the importance of faithful spiritual practice.

I want to thank each person whose story appears here. I would like to acknowledge other people interviewed whose stories are not included but nevertheless enriched the book: Margaret Benefiel, Molly Duplisea, Alice Hildebrand, Linda Jenkins, George Lakey, Christina Stevens, Sas Carey, Sara Hubner, Allison Randall, and Margaret Frazer. I am particularly grateful to Virginia Schonwald and Mary Hillas who read and commented upon each chapter as it was written. I wish to thank readers Sandra Cronk, Marty Grundy, Nancy Lukens, Catherine Whitmire, Judith Favor, Evie Hoffmann, Norton Lyman, Linda Jenkins, and Rita Weathersby, who offered suggestions and made editorial comments. Special thanks to Marty Grundy for writing the foreword. I'm grateful to Rebecca Kratz Mays, editor, for her encouragement from the beginning as well as for her work with Eve Beehler to design the book and bring it to completion. For all these people, for those who have held this process in prayer, and most of all for the unseen guiding hand of the living God, I am grateful.

—Charlotte Fardelmann

Introduction

Give over thine own willing, give over thine own running, give over thine own desiring to know or be anything, and sink down to the seed which God sows in thy heart and let it be in thee, and grow in thee, and breathe in thee, and act in thee, and thou shalt find by sweet experience that the Lord knows that and loves and owns that, and will lead it to the inheritance of life, which is his portion.
—Isaac Penington
17th century Quaker

This is a book of stories from the lives of people seeking to recognize and follow the leadings of God. A leading is the experience of being persistently and insistently drawn towards doing something, or following a certain path in life with a sense that this prompting comes from divine guidance. Following one's leadings is central to Quaker faith and practice. Friends are advised:

> Take heed, dear Friends, to the promptings of love and truth in your hearts. Trust them as the leadings of God whose Light shows us our darkness and brings us to new life. [1]

In the tradition of Friends, Friends are expected to wait upon the leadings of the Spirit before giving vocal ministry. If a message comes to a participant with the insistence that it be shared, then the Friend will speak it aloud. There may be a further requirement to take some action, to become involved in some particular piece of service for others.

This basic practice is not limited to meeting for worship. The process is the same anywhere and anytime: listen inwardly, seek discernment, and if led to do so, share with the meeting community and possibly take some form of action in the world. Friends expect to encounter these nudges of the Spirit throughout any day, even in dreams at night. The promptings may arise from scripture or from the newspaper. A divine nudge may come through the words of an older person or the smile of a child. A concern may arise while seeing homeless people sleeping in the streets or watching ocean waves at a beach.

One Friend, George Gorman, describes his experience this way:

> I would hesitate to claim that I receive direct guidance from God—I do not hear a divine voice that tells me what to do. But I do have a sense that I am being drawn to take one course of action rather than another. The guidance, however, arises from a count-

less number of experiences, influences, attitudes, and disciplines which I have accumulated over the years and upon which I have reflected. [2]

The initial stage of a leading is subtle and inward. One eighteenth-century Friend, John Woolman, felt drawn to take a trip to visit a Native American village during the French and Indian War when it was dangerous to travel in this direction. Woolman described in his journal that initial impulse:

> Love was the first motion, and then a concern arose to spend some time with the Indians, that I might feel and understand their life, and the Spirit they live in, if haply I might receive some instruction from them, or they be in any degree helped forward by my following the leadings of Truth amongst them. And as it pleased the Lord to make way for my going at a time when the troubles of war were increasing, and when by reason of much wet weather travelling was more difficult than usual at that season, I looked upon it as a more favourable opportunity to season my mind and bring me into a nearer sympathy with them.[3]

The next step for Woolman was to bring his concern to his Friends meeting for prayerful consideration. Only after his meeting united with his concern did he set out. He did not go alone but took a Friend with him, another traditional practice of Friends traveling in the ministry.

Many leadings begin with small acts of service, tiny promptings of love and truth. Someone feels compelled to bring soup to a person who is sick or to speak truth when one is tempted to keep quiet about some evil. These spirit-led actions can be just as important to God as more publicly-recognized service. Isaac Penington in 1665 wrote this advice to a friend:

> Do not look for such great matters to begin with . . . thou must join in with the beginnings of life, and be exercised with the day of small things, before

thou meet with the great things, wherein is the clearness and satisfaction of the soul.[4]

It is common practice for Quakers to ask one's meeting for help in discernment and support for a leading. In most cases, there is need not only for discernment and prayer but also for practical assistance and often financial support. One does not usually follow a leading alone. Some people are led to be the supportive ones in the leadings that come to others. As the Spirit works through a number of people, the community is strengthened. As God uses a meeting, church, or spiritual community to lift up the individual's concern and leading, other people may be drawn into the work. The expanded project may grow into a larger ministry far beyond the scope of the individual's original leading.

People in this book refer to the One who leads by a number of names, including "God," "Christ," Lord," and "Spirit." I use the term "leading" to refer to a specific assignment with a beginning and presumably an ending. Often, however, the ending is illusory, for the leading changes form and goes on. In cases where there is a deeper quality which underlies many leadings I may refer to it as a "calling." For example, Jackie Coren, in chapter XII, has a leading to study at Westminster Choir college; her lifelong calling is to lead groups in singing.

To support the process of discernment, Friends are urged to be cautious not to respond to too many leadings at once. To be caught up in too many tasks at once and to be feeling harassed is not God's way. As one centers down in prayer, the Spirit may put one's list of tasks in proper perspective and right priority.

Thomas Kelly, a twentieth-century Friend, wrote:

> Too many of us have too many irons in the fire. We get distracted by the intellectual claims to our interest in a thousand and one good things, and before we know it we are pulled and hauled breathlessly

along by an over-burdened program of good committees and good undertakings. The concern-oriented life is ordered and organized from within. And we learn to say "No" as well as "Yes" by attending to the guidance of inner responsibility. Quaker simplicity needs to be expressed not merely in dress and architecture and height of tombstones but also in the structure of a relatively simplified and coordinated life-program of social responsibilities. [5]

The first way a meeting or church can help an individual who senses a leading is through a corporate process of discernment. How does one know whether or not this leading comes from God? Each person whose story is told here participated in a clearness committee with members of his or her meeting or faith community. In discernment, Friends test the authenticity of a leading looking for these signs.

A spiritual leading from God will:

1. Lead to expressing love and light. A true leading will move in the direction of a transformed life that expresses more love and light, a life that is God-centered rather than ego-centered, a life that expresses one's highest Self rather than one's ego-driven self, a life in harmony with all creation. The first step actually may be a step away from something else. Often one must say "no" before one discovers when to say "yes." There may also be recognition that a certain path into which one is stepping is not right.

2. Come with clarity. A leading may come with such clarity that it cannot be denied. One simply knows that this is what one is supposed to do. It feels right. It fits into one's whole life and fits with other leadings one has been given. In other cases the clarity grows gradually over a period of time. Lucy McIver, in chapter III, comments on her reaction when a woman told her she,

Lucy, was to do more dancing: "She looked right into my heart and I knew she was right."

3. Resonate with one's deepest desires. A true leading touches a deep level in oneself. It resonates on the level with our deepest desires. When we talk about it to others, we show excitement. Although it may frighten us and make our lives less comfortable, we recognize that to move ahead on this impulse is what we are drawn to do. There is a further resonance with the good of others around us, the community, the world, and God's will as we know it.

4. Not be ego-driven. A leading may take us into places we never thought we would choose to go. In traditional language, it is "a cross to my will," meaning it is not something my ego chose. Fear, even terror, often surfaces when one recognizes what one has to do: fear of quitting the job, of moving to a foreign land, of facing the disapproval of one's peers, or of making a fool of oneself-a fool for God. Often it is fear of not being worthy enough to do what is going to be required. Barbara Bazett, in chapter XIV, feels unsure of herself when first appointed to represent Quakers on the World Council of Churches. She is told:

> A sense of inadequacy in a call should not stop you because basically it is based on pride. You just have to trust God. So you don't look as good as you would like to look; (yet) God will get the work done through you.

5. Be persistent. A true leading repeats itself. When in doubt, one is advised to wait. Just as in meeting for worship the impulse to speak will come again and again, stronger each time, so a true leading will repeat itself until we follow it. We must not, however, ignore too long the promptings of the Spirit or we may experience unwanted

consequences. We may find our lives feeling meaning-less and without vitality. It is my experience that at some point in the spiritual journey, there are only two choices, to follow God's will or to be miserable. John Calvi, in chapter X, feels he must go work with AIDS patients. He states: "I had to go do it."

6. Be in harmony with Jesus. An authentic leading will be in harmony with the essence of the life and teachings of Jesus, taken as a whole. A question might be asked: "What would Jesus do?" An authentic leading will be also in harmony with all great spiritual teachings. The lives of great spiritual teachers teach of patience and forgiveness. God calls us to be faithful, not necessarily to be successful. There are frustrations and disappoint-ments, experiences that seem like failure and dead ends. In chapter IX Elaine Bishop struggles with the refusal of the Canadian government to hear and respond to the grievance of indigenous people. Tom Goodridge, in chapter VII, agonized over the destruction of the Garden of Love.

7. Be confirmed by others. Confirmation of a leading will come from joining with other faithful people to wait on the Spirit in holy expectancy. A clearness committee is a Quaker method of finding discernment based upon the trust that when a group of faithful people gather in prayer to seek guidance. Confirmation of a way for-ward may come through reaching feelings of clarity unity, affirmation, and joy. Jesus told us, "Where two or three are gathered in my name, there I am in the midst of them" (Matthew 18:20 KJV). The presence of the Spirit is often felt in such a gathering. Mentors may be extremely powerful influences. Faith Lowell, in chapter VI, feels very close to the woman who led her into work with prisoners.

8. Lead into service to others. Although a leading initially may take a person on an inward journey, in which the primary focus is spiritual growth and transformation, healing, or education for the individual, a true leading leads eventually into service to others. Jill Horton-Lyons and Jim Lyons, the farmers in chapter V, go beyond raising animals to teaching neighborhood children how to care for animals. Kathryn Damiano, a contemplative whose story is in chapter IV, prays for other people and teaches others how to live this life of prayer. Martha Penzer, after her pilgrimage described in chapter VIII, remains in eastern Europe to teach high school youth in Slovenia.

9. Require rest. The depth of love and light in a leading sustains a person in the face of trial, but often the intensity of service one is called to do simply requires rest in order not to burnout. Several of the people in this book experience burnout from the intense social and political activism required by their leadings. Pamela Meidell in chapter XIII describes the need to pause in her life of activism and take time out to recover her energy and commitment.

10. Lead to more love, joy, peace, and patience. There may be misery as a person begins this walk with God. One may be faced with giving up parts of one's life that one loves. But as one moves deeper into a more God-centered life, there is a growing sense of the fruits of faithful service. In time, after years of faithfulness, a person gradually develops in the ability to become more patient, to love with more compassion, to feel more joy in small everyday occurrences, and to be rooted in inner peace. A person who has persisted in spiritual faithfulness for many years will often show signs of the biblical fruits of the Spirit, "love, joy, peace, patience, kindness, goodness, faithfulness, gentleness, and self-control" (Galations 5:22-23 NIV).

A leading has a life of its own that can guide in the choice's of one's responsibilities. A leading grows organically, like a tree. There are stages in the life of a leading. The first motion may be a concern that remains persistent. A time of mulling it over usually follows, a time of inward searching within the individual. Following this is the time for sharing with those closest to the individual—a spouse or a few close friends and select persons from one's faith community. When a fresh leading is first tested it is like a seedling coming out of the ground; it is a vulnerable time. It is possible for a small plant to be stepped on before it gains the strength to stand alone. This is the time when the leading needs encouragement. Support may come from friends, family members, mentors, or other helpers. This is often the time when a person applies to a foundation for grants to begin the work.

Further along, after the initial phase is over, there may be a long period of faithfully doing the work. The work may shift in direction from time to time, still following the basic leading. The intensity of a leading may bring a person into burnout. There will be need for rest and a period of reflection, of catching up inwardly with the outward experiences. Many people take retreats and work on healing themselves before return to the work.

A leading may not go forward in the way one expects. There may be leadings that seem to be dead ends and make one wonder what could be the lesson to be learned. It may take years before the meaning becomes clear.

After a while the person may no longer feel the press of this particular leading. The particular task may be completed. Even if it is not completed, this may be time to turn over the work to other people. To make this transition gracefully takes care and discernment.

In this book the stories represent many kinds of leadings and illustrate different stages of the process of following a leading. Each story gives light on a particular aspect of the process.

I hope that these stories will touch the heart, will inspire readers to listen more closely to the still, small voice within, and give them the courage to respond to God calling.

—Charlotte Fardelmann

Notes

1. *Quaker Faith and Practice, Yearly Meeting of the Religious Society of Friends in Britain,* Warwick, England, 1955, Chapter 26, Section 226.01 (Advices #1).

2. George Gorman, *The Amazing Fact of Quaker Worship* (Swarthmore Lecture) (London: Quaker Home Service, 1973), p. 71.

3. *The Journal and Major Essays of John Woolman,* ed. Phillips P. Moulton (Richmond, Indiana: Friends United Press, 1971), pp. 127-28 (journal entry for 12 vi 1763).

4. Isaac Penington, *Letters,* ed. John Barclay, 1828, pp. 213-14 (Letter LXIV to Bridget Atley, dated 1665).

5. Thomas Kelly, *The Testament of Devotion* (New York: Harper, 1941), p. 110.

I. SEED MONEY

Charlotte Lyman Fardelmann

Charlotte Fardelmann

Create in me a clean heart, O God;
and renew a right spirit within me.
Cast me not away from thy presence;
and take not thy holy spirit from me.
Restore unto me the joy of thy salvation;
and uphold me with thy free spirit.

Psalm 51:10-12 (KJV)

*M*y home stands at the confluence of two rivers near enough to their ocean mouth to be filled by the strong currents of the salt sea tides twice a day. Beside the river stands an oak tree whose roots are licked by salt water at high tide and whose branches are low enough to climb.

This tree planted by the river reminds me of the psalmist's words describing a person who walks in Godly ways:

> And he shall be like a tree planted by the rivers of water, that bringeth forth his fruit in his season; his leaf also shall not wither; and whatever he doeth shall prosper.
>
> *Psalm 1:2-3 (KJV)*

Sometimes I sit under my tree and gaze at the river, imagining it as the river of life. Each of us is out there paddling our own tiny kayak, canoe, or other craft. We paddle to the left or to the right. We paddle faster and slower. We feel as if we are in control.

If one could stand back, high up on the river bank, however, one could see that our tiny boats are being carried by strong currents which carry us in ways we do not understand nor even recognize. The river is strewn with whirlpools and rocks. From this perspective, clearly we are not in control. A deeper current carries us along in safety, the divine current whose source is God.

This is my story about launching out into the current of God. I was fifty-six years old at the time, living in my comfortable old home on the river. My husband and I had been divorced for many years and my four children were grown.

I worked as a free-lance journalist and photographer for magazines and newspapers and had just completed my first book, Islands Down East, a tour guide to the islands of Maine and New Hampshire. In the middle of writing this tour guide it became clear to me that when the book was finished I was to turn my attention to my spiritual journey. I turned from writing about other people and places, from

outward islands, and began to focus on my personal relationship with God. I spent the following year at Pendle Hill,
a Quaker Center in Pennsylvania where people come for
study, creation, reflection, and contemplation in service to
God and others.

One focus of my year was dealing with money. Money is a
resource one needs to consider on any spiritual journey. One
of the most common reactions to being nudged by the Spirit
is, "There's no way I can do that; I don't have the money!"
Money is an emotional issue no matter how much money one
has. It is not easy to ask for money. It can cause the person
requesting money to feel vulnerable and needy. There can be
issues of guilt and anxiety for the person asked as well. One
question may be: "How far out on a limb does God want me
to go?" "God will provide," we are told. But sometimes God
waits until the last minute. What about providing for old
age? Is it right to set a limit on God's leading beyond which
one does not feel comfortable going? How does one deal with
anxiety in the face of certain promptings of the still, small
voice?

In this chapter I focus on the other side of the coin, donating seed money for people to take the next step on their spiritual journey. It is my story of being nudged by the Spirit to
put inherited wealth into creating a fund primarily to support Quakers in following the leadings of God. The grants
our fund provide are only a drop in the bucket for most of
these people. That drop may be a significant one, however,
and come at the time when it is badly needed. It can provide encouragement to take the next step.

Our board members also pray for these people and hold
them and their leadings in the Light. Grant recipients sometimes say this prayer is more important than the money.
It can be a long, lonely journey out there following God's
leading. The board operates by the principles of Friends business practices, holding meetings in a worshipful mode,
seeking God's will on decisions. Once a year grant recipi-

ents are invited to a gathering at which they can share their life journeys with each other and with board members.

The founders of the fund have been overwhelmed by the blessings they have received, illustrating the truth of the words of Jesus:

> Give and it will be given to you. A good measure, pressed down, shaken together, and running over, will be poured into your lap. For the same measure that you use, it will be measured to you.
>
> Luke 6:38 (NIV)

The importance of giving whatever one can give is part of the teachings in many, if not all, religions. Generosity seems to be built into God's laws—God's generosity towards us and our response of generosity towards others.

Jon Kabat-Zinn, writing from a Buddhist perspective in **Wherever You Go There You Are** *(pp. 62, 64)*, advises :

> See if you can be in touch with a core within you which is rich beyond reckoning in all important ways. Let that core start radiating its energy outwardly, through your entire body, and beyond. Experiment with giving away this energy—in little ways at first—directing it towards yourself and towards others with no thought of gain or return. Give more than you think you can, trusting that you are richer than you think. . . . I'm not talking solely of money or material possessions, although it can be wonderfully growth-enhancing, uplifting and truly helpful to share material abundance. Rather what is being suggested here is that you practice sharing the fullness of your being, your best self, your enthusiasm, your vitality, your spirit, your trust, your openness, above all, your presence. Share it with yourself, with your family, with the world. See what happens—especially to you. You may find that you gain a greater

*clarity about your relationships, as well as more en-
ergy rather than less. You may find that, rather than
exhausting your resources, you will replenish them.
Such is the power of mindful selfless generosity. At
the deepest level, there is no giver, no gift and no
recipient . . . only the universe rearranging itself.*

My story is about wrestling with the issues of inherited
money and the questions it raises. What doth the Lord
require? How much do I give? To whom do I give? And how
do I give it? How will giving affect one's relationship
with others?

Exploring Spiritual Journey

My year at Pendle Hill was surprisingly transformative.
Through a variety of classes, friendships, and working with
a spiritual consultant, my spiritual life deepened. I began to
walk with God in a more personal way.

At the same time I became more open to the shadow side
of myself. One aspect of this shadow was a growing unease
about inherited wealth. Growing up during the depression in
an upper-class home, I attended a small private day school
for girls. I had always felt different from most people, isolated from the mainstream of life. Although I was a fairly
contented child who loved her parents and friends, deep
inside I was estranged from the high-society world in which
I grew up. I disliked the prejudice, the showy parties, the
formal gowns, and the social drinking. My father never encouraged me to work. As was common with people of wealth
in his time, he thought one should take care of daughters
until they married. He worked hard at investing his money
and passing it along to his children and grandchildren.

I graduated from college before I had to think about
earning money. Even then, living with friends in New York
City, I had some income from stocks and bonds to supple-

ment what I made at work. Although this cushion of money helped me at crisis times in my life, it also made trouble for me all along the line. As a young woman I did not have a strong incentive to earn money so I never developed a career. When my husband became financially successful, I didn't fully appreciate it. This difference in attitude towards money contributed to our divorce.

Money also affected friendships. After I was divorced a close companion told me she no longer could be my friend because she had to work to earn her family's income and I didn't. Because inherited money seemed to cause trouble, I generally hid it and learned not to mention it to friends. I even hid it from myself by hiring an investment manager to look after it for me. When I kept this experience hidden and secret, it only made me miserable. It was late in life that I began to look at this secret. I opened to God's transformative power which turned those negative feelings into positive action in the world.

One basic conflict in my mind paralyzed me. On the one hand my father, who had died several years before, had told me, "Don't spend or give away principal. Use the income and keep the principal to pass down in the family." On the other hand I felt the injustice of having more money and resources than did the people around me.

As I watched my friends struggle with their deepest yearnings, their nudges from the Spirit, their dreams of making a difference in the world, a concern arose in me to provide financial support for people in this situation, to help empower them to do God's work in the world.

As I pondered how my spiritual journey seemed to differ from the journeys of other people I knew, I began to understand that no two spiritual journeys are the same. I began to imagine life as a big scavenger hunt. Each of us looks for a clue, finds it, and moves on in another direction towards another clue. My problem comes when I watch my friend finding a clue and think my friend's clue is my clue. Each of us is on a unique path. These paths, however, intertwine. We play bit parts, and sometimes bigger parts, in each other's plays.

Acknowledging My Wealth and Beginning to Share it

Over the years, I also attended conferences for people with inherited wealth. These conferences focused on dealing with emotional issues around inheritance and offered practical information on how to make a positive influence in the world. As I attended these conferences and worked with my issues, feelings began to surface and become resolved. It was amazingly healing to sit with seventy people who dared to share with each other their hidden secrets about money.

I began to see that I was tied as if by a thick cable to my father's expectations. Gradually, as I learned how to shift my financial resources into ethical investments and began to make larger charitable gifts, this cable was being lifted off my shoulders.

I began to take steps that felt right, in spite of the fact—at first—that they were generally not what I wanted to do. On some deeper level, however, they were precisely what I wanted to do. I was doing what would heal me. Following this inwardly guided path was lifting the cable that was binding me. It was like walking through a fog in which you cannot see very far ahead. As I completed one task, the next task would appear.

Expanding My "Family"

It gradually became clear to me that my sense of "family" was expanding. It was beginning to go beyond blood relatives to include Quakers and other people on the spiritual path. In a deeper way, I have begun to feel the interconnection with all people, animals, and life on this planet.

One experience which began to free me to be my authentic self was taking part in political action, traveling to Nicaragua with Witness for Peace during the Contra War in 1987. Our delegation visited a town which had been attacked by Contra forces a month before we came. The school teacher was killed. Many others were killed or wounded. We were asked to lead a memorial service for those who had died. This trip opened my eyes and my heart to the people there.

A few years later I had the privilege of staying with Kenyan Quakers in East Africa. The strong faith of my hosts taught me much. The sound of my African Friends singing "More about Jesus" still reverberates within me.

A third life-changing trip was visiting a small mountain village in central Mexico where a Quaker organization, Right Sharing of World Resources, had helped to fund a water project. The local people showed us the results—water pumped up to their mountain homes. They were glad we had come to appreciate what they had accomplished. At a celebratory feast, we rejoiced together and thanked God.

These experiences changed my perspective on the oppression that goes on between the rich, powerful people and the poor, weak people of the world. Despite the suffering caused by this oppression, these people taught me a different way to look at poverty and riches. I met people who had little material wealth but were rich in faith, love, and joy.

To go on these trips was to follow my deepest leadings. I was beginning to move beyond my father's understandings, beyond the thinking of the narrow world of my childhood. By the time I got up my nerve to be arrested at the Nevada Test Site, protesting the testing of nuclear bombs, I had cut loose from family expectations. I was freed up to decide for myself whether or not to give over a portion of my inherited principal. Since that time my giving has increased.

Creating A Fund

Mary Hillas, Barbara Potter, and I created a fund through which we could give money primarily to Quakers who were faithfully seeking to follow divine leadings. We told people that we intended to do this and waited for God to reveal the next step. Soon we had proposals. Our organization did not meet in a formal board room. Twice a year we sat down together in "Charlotte's Web," a small shed on Mary and Barbara's property. We held the proposals prayerfully in the Light until we sensed what we were supposed to do. Then we prayed for the grantees during the period of the grant.

One of my spiritual practices is to take "Quiet Days," days with God. It is on those days that I receive my "marching orders." Ideas emerge which have a compelling quality about them. One such idea, a clear leading, was that I was to be in touch with the grantees as much as possible. We asked for reports from the grantees. I began to visit some of them. The three of us were overwhelmed with awe, gratitude, and joy as we read these reports and learned more from my visits. My feelings about my inheritance began to shift from feeling like a millstone to feeling like a gift.

It was at this time we realized how giving and receiving are one. When a gift is given in the right spirit, it is a gift to the receiver. When a gift is received in the right spirit, appreciatively, this becomes a gift to the giver. Looking at this interaction, it becomes impossible to identify who is giver and who is receiver. Like the yin-yang parts of a circle, giving and receiving are both parts of one whole. The interaction is a sign of God's manifesting in the world. It is whole— and holy.

Furthermore, as the recipient takes the grant and puts it to work in God's service, and as people involved in that service are moved to help others, the gift goes on and on.

Dipping Into Principal

The next phase in my own spiritual journey was seven years after we started the fund. We decided to form a non-profit organization. I had a personal struggle around making a substantial gift of principal to the new foundation.

I had three nudges on this issue. The first one happened the night before our new corporation's first board meeting. I was anxious about how much capital to transfer to the new organization. I asked in prayer for a sign. In the morning I awoke with a song in my head:

> *"Tis the spring of souls today.*
> *Christ has burst his prison."*

I had not sung this hymn for twenty years since I left the Episcopal Church to become a Friend. I recognized this hymn as the processional used for the Easter morning service at the Episcopal church in Portsmouth I used to attend. I sang in the choir, my daughters sang in junior choir, and my sons were acolytes. The procession went down the aisle around the congregation and back up the aisle, led by a deacon swinging incense. It was a glorious celebratory event.

As I listened to the song in my head that morning, I realized that I had been imprisoned by my own attitudes about inherited wealth. Now I was being given a chance to be freed.

This vision gave me the first boost towards the decision to donate to the new fund enough capital so it could generate income for grants and so the fund could go on after I and the other present donors pass away.

The second nudge had to do with my physical body yet it was related to my inner struggle of giving up control, one of life's major lessons. When a person is struggling with inner issues, there is often a physical component.

During the period I was thinking about this decision, I had one physical trauma after another. First I broke my writing arm and then I pulled a leg tendon. The leg bothered me so much on a sailing cruise that I had to return home by wheelchair. Throughout this period I was aware that there was a spiritual component to the physical trauma. It felt as if I was being prepared for something new. I felt strangely peaceful inside.

Following this came six weeks of a debilitating cough. A week before the first gathering of the recipients of the fund's grants, I went to my osteopath in desperation. My doctor suggested the cough might have a message for me. "Don't forget to ask the question," he advised as I went out the door of his office. After meditating on it, I realized the message was: "Cough it up."

The third nudge was this: I took a retreat in preparation for the gathering. The retreat director suggested I visualize myself in a Bible story. The story I chose was the loaves and the fishes. I was a little girl and my mother had given me some money to go to the store to buy bread. After buying five loaves and stuffing them into my knapsack, I fished in a creek and caught two fishes. On my way home I came upon a huge crowd of people at the foot of a mountain. A man with a deep, resonant voice was speaking. His voice attracted me so I went over and sat next to him. Although the words did not mean much to me, I enjoyed the warmth of his presence. It felt good to be near this man, whose name was Jesus.

When Jesus stopped speaking people around him said, "it is getting near dinner time; send the people to the villages around here to get food." Jesus said, "Maybe someone has food." I thought about giving him my bread but my mother would get mad at me if I came home empty handed. I thought, "Maybe I could give him two or three loaves?" Then our eyes met. His bright blue eyes carried a depth I had not seen before in anyone. He said, "TRUST ME" (accent on trust). He was saying with his eyes, "Just wait till you see; this is going to be wonderful."

So I gave him all of it, all five loaves and two fishes. He broke the bread and fish into tiny bits and as he broke them, the bits expanded into huge chunks. Then he broke off bits of those chunks and they expanded. There was plenty to feed everyone and lots left over. I filled my knapsack full to take home to my mother.

When I came out of this visualization I remembered the look in Jesus' eyes and his words, "Trust me." He was inviting me to participate in a miracle. The words, "Trust me," remind me of the trust it takes to set out on the ocean for a night sea journey. I may have anxiety in going out into unknown waters until I remember that I am always held in the everlasting arms of God, cradled in the deep sea of the Spirit. Those nudges pushed me over the edge. I donated several hundred thousand dollars to our new non-profit fund. The income from this added to the amount donated by other founders was enough for several grants at each of the semi-annual grant sessions.

Blessings

The miracle has already begun. The board members and donors have been awed by the stories of what the grantees have done with the grants received. The love will go on, the projects continue long after the grants were given. Grantees have created songs, massaged torture victims, bridged chasms between people of different cultures, taught disturbed inner city children, sat with dying patients, mediated family difficulties, protected our environment, created art, studied at spiritual centers, written books, led choirs, healed the sick, and prepared themselves for service to others. In all this, we have experienced a miracle as wonderful as the Bible story. The annual gatherings for grant recipients were conceived as a way of celebrating this miracle by giving the grantees a chance to hear each others' stories.

At the first gathering of recipients, I had a vision that I entered the tree of life and found many people within it, each sitting with a seed. The seeds represented the divine leadings that people sit with until they can figure out how to put them into action. The fund offers a way to help people nurture their "seeds."

This journey has led me from guilt to gratitude and from isolation to community. Instead of feeling we are giving money away, I feel we are investing in people. Thinking about what the recipients have done with the grants, I realize the benefits go on and on. Each of these people is nurturing more seeds as they serve others.

I like to think I have a part in each project. To the creators of these projects, I say:

> When I see your angel wall hanging, I can imagine myself as a thread in it. When you are writing your book, my prayers are that you can find your words. When you walk along a muddy path in Guatemala, I walk with you.

II. SPIRITUAL DISCERNMENT

William and Frances Taber

photo by Mary Gabel

Fran and Bill Taber

*And we know that all things work together
for good to them that love God, to them that
are the called according to his purpose.*

Romans 8:28 (KJV)

M arch rains are hitting Ohio when I stop to visit William and Frances Taber in their Barnesville home. It is dusk, and Fran has dinner ready. We settle into a short time of worship at the table. Fran serves tofu stew made with their own garden vegetables, rutabagas, parsnips, carrots, and potatoes, along with home-baked biscuits. A fire blazes in the fireplace behind me. I feel warmed by the meal, the fire, and the hospitality of these friends.

Bill is 69 and Fran is about to turn 67. They have recently retired from working at Pendle Hill, a Quaker center for study and service near Philadelphia where Bill taught Quaker Studies and Fran managed the retreat program. Now they have returned to their home in Barnesville, next door to Olney Friends School where they worked before they went to Pendle Hill. The couple has owned this house since 1959 before their children were born. A large garden area behind the house provides much of the food this couple consumes. The vegetables from the previous summer are being eaten tonight. Fran remarks that it is almost time to plant the peas. Seed catalogues lie on the hall table.

I got to know both Bill and Fran when I was a student and visiting teacher at Pendle Hill. I took a number of courses from Bill and was grateful for this opportunity. I always enjoyed his classes, his deeply mystical spirituality, the twinkle in his eye, his good humor and creative methods of teaching. For one course called "Traveling in the Ministry," he arranged for small groups of us to visit local Quaker families to have what he called "an opportunity," a time for prayer. Many times when I had questions about a spiritual experience, it was Bill who took the time to listen, to pray with me, and to advise me. I grew close to Fran as well, for we shared the love of personal retreats. It was Fran who prepared me, when I was a student, for a retreat in the Spring House in which I had a profound spiritual experience.

Living in a center such as Pendle Hill can be wearing as well as wonderful. The community, with all its intensity, is *always with you. Sometimes it is important to take a break. The leading for which Bill and Fran received a grant from the Lyman Fund was simply to take a Sabbath Year, during the school year of 1989-90, at their home in Barnesville, Ohio. The Tabers' sabbath year included daily time of retirement as well as longer silent retreats.*

Sabbath time is part of the Judeo-Christian tradition, beginning with the Creation story in Genesis when God rested on the seventh day, "And on the seventh day God ended his work which he had made; and he rested on the seventh day from all his work which he had made. And God blessed the seventh day, and sanctified it: because that in it he had rested from all his work which God created and made." Genesis 2:2-3 (KJV).

The life of Jesus demonstrated a rhythm between active service and rest; he took time in the midst of teaching to the crowds to find a quiet spot in which to pray.

Quakers traditionally have referred to this as "retirement"—time set aside for being with God, for resting in the divine Presence. In her Pendle Hill Pamphlet, Come Aside and Rest Awhile *(p. 5), Fran quotes from Howard Brinton's* Friends for 300 Years *(p. 135):*

> *Retirement is considered by the Quakers as a "Christian duty." The members, therefore, of this Religious Society are expected to wait in silence, not only in their places of worship, but occasionally in their families or in their private chambers, in the intervals of their daily occupations, that in stillness of heart, and in freedom from the active contrivance of their own will, they may acquire both direction and strength for the performance of the duties of life.*

The Taber's story focuses on spiritual discernment of how to use this sabbath year. Patricia Loring describes this inward process in her Pendle Hill Pamphlet Spiritual Discernment (p. 3):

Discernment is the faculty we use to distinguish the true movement of the Spirit to speak in meeting for worship from the wholly human urge to share, to instruct or to straighten people out. It is the capacity we exercise in a centered meeting for worship for the conduct of business to sense the right course for the meeting to take in complex or difficult circumstances. It is the ability to see into people, situations, and possibilities to identify what is of God in them and what is of the numerous other sources in ourselves—and what may be both. It is that fallible intuitive gift we use in attempting to discriminate the course to which we are personally led by God in a given situation, from other impulses and from the generalized judgments of conscience.

Throughout the sabbath year the Tabers discerned as carefully as they could how to use their time and energy. This story illustrates how these contemporary Friends go about the practice of spiritual discernment.

*B*ill and Fran speak with quiet, gentle voices, addressing each other as "thee," in the manner of Conservative Friends. The Tabers are both "birthright" Conservative Friends, born and brought up in that tradition. They are often asked to interpret this tradition to outsiders. The term "Conservative" does not refer to the political right wing. The Tabers explain that it refers to a branch of Quakerism which seeks to conserve the values of simplicity, pacifism, and strong sense of putting the community ahead of one's self. Conservative Friends have maintained the unprogrammed worship of the original Friends in seventeenth-century England. They have also maintained the strong Christian orientation of classical Quakerism. Many of these Friends are farmers, living close to the earth. Conservative Friends meetings are located primarily in Ohio, Iowa, and North Carolina.

Part of my reason for being here is to have a retreat at the Tabers' home. The simple orderliness of their home, the relaxed pace, and the warm hospitality invited me into a meditative mode. I soak in the times of quiet reflection and deep silent worship. In the evening around 9:00 p.m., the Tabers invite me to join them in their evening devotions. We settle into comfortable chairs beside the wood stove for a time of quiet. Fran reads a short devotional passage and then invites me to join them in considering the day, to ask to be shown what is significant, and to come up with a high point, a blessing, and a low point which I might want to share towards the end of the worship time. As we sit together in the silence and then share from our day's experience, I feel grounded in the Spirit and wonderfully prepared for the night's rest.

After our worship, Bill says, "I remember long ago in this house, we used to light two candles on the mantle and turn out all the lights, having a time of quiet together at the end of the day, after the children were in bed. I don't know how faithful we were to that custom, probably not as faithful as I like to remember it."

Fran comments, "Probably not." She adds, "Turning out all the lights and doing this by candlelight achieves the purpose of quieting the atmosphere and letting the clutter be less obvious."

"We do currently have this time of quiet before retiring," she continues. "We have not been consistent with that through the years, but we are being pretty consistent with it right now. We have the feeling that over a period of time this practice will bring to consciousness things about ourselves that we need to encourage, things about ourselves that require more learning, watching, or correcting." Fran says that occasionally one of them, usually Bill, offers a vocal prayer.

Next morning I notice Bill, dressed in red checked wool shirt and blue jeans, putting wood into the stoves which heat the house. After the living room stove begins to crackle, Bill settles in a chair nearby for his personal devotion time. Fran joins us and we all take time for reading and quiet meditation together. In front of the window, Fran's amaryllis plant is sporting four deep red blossoms.

After our quiet time, I inquire about Bill's and Fran's usual morning practice. Bill says, "For quite a while I have been reading something from the gospels and then reading from the epistles. I would just keep going through both the epistles and then the gospels. Then I would have a time of quiet, ideally about a twenty-minute space of contemplative prayer followed by intercessory prayer. Those time limits vary a lot. I feel as if I have missed something if I don't have this."

Fran says, "I started using an Episcopal lexicon, using the scripture readings from that and followed that for a number of years. At the present time I am varying that. I usually read a psalm or two and a New Testament passage, usually from the Gospels. I'll also often include a bit of devotional reading from some other source, as well as a time of quiet waiting and a bit of intercessory prayer. Occasionally I will write in my journal."

At this point she turns to Bill and comments, "Thee writes in thy journal sometimes."

Bill responds, "Yes. I don't write in it as often as I used to, but it varies a lot. I don't do it at any specific time but as I feel moved to do so."

We move into the kitchen for breakfast—granola, an apple, and Fran's freshly baked muffins. She offers her homemade peach butter.

Over breakfast, I ask them about other spiritual disciplines. Bill tells about a weekly practice they have had for some time. He says, "We started it when we were at Pendle Hill, the first year on staff, so it has lasted now for some fourteen or fifteen years."

Fran interjects a point for accuracy, "With some lapses with circumstances, but we always come back to it."

Bill continues, "Over our traditional popcorn supper on Sunday night we would be spiritual friends for each other. I would listen to Fran first, listen to her talk about her spiritual journey during the week, whatever she felt was important to share, and when she would get through I would share my story. Now, sometimes it would seem to Fran that I need to go first, but mostly we did it that way."

At this point Fran explains why she goes first:

> The reason we started out with me going first was because there was a natural tendency or habitual pattern between us that made it easier for Bill to go on and on talking about himself and easier for me to listen. So we decided by reversing this, and forcing me to start talking first even though I felt I had to get over some kind of hump to do it, this was good. I would do it first and then Bill follow. That does not seem important as much of the time now, sometimes we do it one way and sometimes the other.

Bill remarks: "Fran is bolder now and also more accustomed to reaching into herself and saying what she feels. Words have always been easy for me. And I have always been interested in inner states and that sort of thing."

A Sabbath Year

I asked Bill and Fran to reflect upon their sabbath year. What did a "sabbath year" mean to them? What projects did they undertake? How did they discern how to use this time? What effect did this sabbath year have on each of them?

The sabbatical leave began in August. Bill and Fran lived in the upstairs of their home in Barnesville, Ohio, so that they could rent the lower floor for income. There was an outside stairway to their floor. They turned their bedroom into a living room, used a hot plate for a stove, and carried water from the bathroom.

Fran wrote in a letter late in November:

> Our upstairs three rooms are now a comfortable nest and workplace, filled at appropriate intervals with the smells of food cooking. When my creative impulses get channeled into cooking, they take off and I need to pull in the reins to get at something else. As the weeks go by, now that things are in order, we are learning gradually to sink deeper into that feeling of spaciousness, inner and outer, which is one of the things the year is meant to provide.
>
> The other thing the year is meant to provide, of course, is time for reading and writing. I have done a lot of background reading for my project, and have now got out some piles of old letters which I am eager to get into. Bill was rattling his typewriter this afternoon, working on a second or third draft of an article destined for the Friends Journal.
>
> Bill, not surprisingly, has gone through layers of fatigue since we've been here. I think he's bottomed out and is gaining energy now. Both of us in varying ways have gone through the "I should be getting more done on my project" stage. We keep returning to the realization that this grounding in our space, this rest, this healing, is a necessary foundation for whatever else is done during the year.
>
> The rightness of being here this particular year is very evident. The school (Olney Friends School) and the Yearly Meeting (Ohio Yearly Meeting Conservative) are in difficult places, and there are ways which seem right for us to relate to the situation—carefully discerned. We are taking care not to become over-involved, you may be sure.

Fran's letter states that she and Bill agreed to do one significant thing, at the invitation of Cleveland meeting. It was to lead an invitational conference called "Dialogue with the Taproot," which will mix Friends from a relatively young meeting with Friends from more seasoned meetings as well as Friends from other parts of Quakerism. Fran explained the process of discernment on whether or not they were to lead this conference. She says, "This is so close to our central passion for trying to help communicate the truth we see inherent in Conservative Quakerism at its best, that our 'yes' to that one invitation came from a very deep place."

The way the Tabers discern whether or not to accept such a leading comes from years of practice. Bill states, "There is the whole process of communication between us, sort of checking back and forth. How does it seem to each of us? We have turned down a number of things, not simply for schedule reasons, but just because we did not feel led to spend our energy in that direction."

Fran describes her discernment process this way: "The way I tend to do on-going life discernment is by keeping an open ear cocked inside as I think about what I'm going to do today, as I think about the focus for the next week, next month, or next year. As Bill and I talk about things, I do it with the feeling that I am listening with an inner ear as to what feels right, what sits well, what feels comfortable. Part of that has to do with what feels in accordance with the on-going movement, on-going flow of my life, of our lives, of what it feels that our lives are most significantly about, what one might think of as overall calling in life."

Fran speaks of the juggling act in which she juggles the on-going themes of her life callings. She has identified Quakerism and spiritual nurture as on-going themes in her life. "These themes interplay around and over the base of our life as a family. Family life, meeting life, the broader meeting community are things that get involved in this spiritual juggling act."

When asked what would happen if one of them had a leading to do one thing and the other had a leading in a different direction, Fran responds, "We've never thought about it that way. Whenever we have considered relocating or changing our situation significantly, we look at it together and try to feel what is right for us as a couple and as a family. This doesn't mean we ignore what each of us is feeling, but the point towards which we are focused is what is right for us as a couple or as a family. As part of looking in that direction, we would look at what each of us feels about staying or changing and how it would affect both the personal life and the vocational life of each of us. As we do that we keep it all wrapped up together, each part being part of the whole."

Bill presents an example of a time when the family had to make such a discernment. The Tabers were living away from their Ohio home while Bill had a temporary job. When Bill was offered a permanent job in the new location, Bill and Fran included the children in the decision. Bill says, "I remember walking in very deep snow trying to get clear in my own mind what was right to do." Bill longed to take the new job. He thought Fran was interested in it too. Bill recalls, "We raised the question with (our daughter) Debora who was ten, going on eleven. It was almost as if she wouldn't speak to us for three days after that. We could tell from her point of view, not going back home was just a terrible thing. If there was a factor that changed the nature of my discernment, that was a very significant one."

Fran adds, "That was really the hardest decision we ever made. It took a great deal of our energy during that winter. We would imagine ourselves into one scenario and see what it felt like. Then we would imagine ourselves into the opposite scenario and see what it felt like. It was as if we couldn't be really comfortable either way. Whichever we decided, some part of us would have regrets. But it was as if we would feel least uncomfortable with returning to Ohio at that time. Anne was ready for her senior year at Olney and Debora had three more years in grade school. It felt right for them to keep their roots here until each of them was ready for another stage in her development."

Olney

Now in their sabbath year, after ten years of teaching and community life at Pendle Hill, they are led to serve the Ohio Yearly Meeting (Conservative). Bill says, "The Yearly Meeting was deeply divided on several major issues. Our own local meeting had deep wounds in it resulting from the way some of these differences had been handled there. Disagreement about the importance of Jesus Christ and the Bible had caused a growth of suspicion which affected the way in which many issues were dealt with."

One of the issues was a proposal to close Olney Friends School, to develop it as a retreat center and to move towards reopening it with a somewhat different emphasis. Olney Friends School is dear to the hearts of both Bill and Fran. Both of them attended this school in their youth. Bill was a teacher and principal there for twenty years. Fran also worked at the school. Bill felt he must do what he could to keep the school going. He says, "The future of Olney and the related theological issues affected everyone throughout the yearly meeting in an energy-consuming way that is hard to imagine unless one has actually lived in the midst of it."

Bill and Fran had been living and working at Pendle Hill, a center which attracts people from varied theological and religious backgrounds, including many liberal Friends. So they were seen as "insider-outsiders" who could listen and interpret different points of view. Bill immediately saw that he could be instrumental in helping people find better ways to communicate. Bill comments, "These conversations—and the many visits, meetings, prayer meetings, and consultations which grew out of them—would add up to a surprising amount of time which we did not begrudge, since we felt that we were in a unique position to be of help as insider-outsiders."

Olney Friends School did not close. The Tabers and many other Friends worked hard on this all year. Bill said, "I could not refuse that service since Providence had placed me there and I was available to help at a time when the school was in a precarious situation."

Bill

Bill often has leadings related to developing creative ways to deal with problem situations. When he sat in on some Olney Friends School board meetings during that sabbath year, there was a general understanding that the board wanted to keep to good Quaker business meeting process. When the meetings veered away from that, it was sometimes Bill who brought them back to center. He had the idea to bring a little bell with him to the meetings, so he could ring it, when appropriate, and that bell would be a reminder for the group to take time to reconnect with its divine center in Christ. Just having the bell sitting there was a reminder, for some people, to keep close to the Spirit.

Bill often has small creative ideas come to him which seem to him a form of God's grace. "I've lived and worked in institutions all my life. Over the years, my gifts and my concern have often been primarily in the field of community, the spiritual aspect of community." He gives an example of when he was a teacher at the Olney Friends School. "At times I would have moments of feeling something was growing fragile in the community and that it was important to meet in worship with just a few people. So I sent out invitations and just a few students and a few teachers would join me in meeting for worship. I did not really know what was wrong. I just had a feeling that the heart of the community needed to be recentered. People often commented on how powerful these meetings were."

At Pendle Hill, Bill did the same thing. He would call for meetings for healing when he felt one was needed. Bill comments, "Community was always my work." He compares it to making a good meal, "I have heard talk about how when you make a good meal, you think about it ahead of time, you work hard on it, then it's all done. The things I would do would not leave a clear record behind them, but that was my work, both at Pendle Hill and at Olney.

The difficult part for Bill is finding himself in the middle between antagonistic people who may attack him verbally. When asked how he deals with that, Bill responds, "What do I do in theory or what do I do in practice?" He says:

> I know what I do in theory. The Bible—Jesus and the epistles—gives plenty of direction on that. When my faithfulness and the grace I'm given is adequate, I can just keep returning to that living center and let it go. But temperamentally it's very difficult not to feel oppressed. Physiologically I can feel it. I am sensitive. I can pick up vibrations even when people are not saying anything. My human reaction is pretty strong. Sometimes I have been inhibited for days after one of these meetings. It would live in my mind.
>
> But recently, I think the thing that has made a difference has been prayers of many people. I have felt myself sustained by a power coming from beyond. If I am willing to become truly dependent and honestly accept the prayer, then there is a letting go. Paradoxically, as I accept and let go, there is room for the work of Christ within. I am able to look more clearly at the light at the center of creation, which again is Christ. So it is difficult and a real exercise and test of faithfulness to keep returning to the living center, what I call "the cross of joy," no matter what happens.

He reflects on this and then says, "But this has been a long process."

A phrase which has helped him is "living in the absorptive mode. " He says, "I am not absorbing it into my body but I am letting it pass through me. This is a kind of prayerful mode."

Although the antagonisms connected with community life can be difficult for Bill, the blessings of Spirit-filled community life make up for it. "The most exciting thing is feeling that Life flowing through the group," he says. "The group is alert and alive and spiritually united through the Holy Spirit." After times like this, Bill is apt to speak of feeling "refreshed."

Monastery

One piece of the sabbath year for Bill was to spend two weeks at a Trappist monastery in Virginia. He says, "I was permitted to live within the walls of the monastery, so I took part in the daily offices, and I worked in the bakery. We were allowed to talk some, but a lot of the time was silent. There was no proscription on speaking, except from after the 7:30 a.m. service until 8:00 a.m., but one was expected not to speak needlessly. I spent time in silence, in my cell, or walking, or in the library.

"It was a very important two weeks there," says Bill. He had stayed there once before and had found it beneficial. He says, "It enables me to get closer to living in the stream all the time. It is hard to explain—there is an integration, and a unity, and a harmony that comes into one's life; one can feel it for a while after one goes back into the world. It is still there."

Four Doors to Meeting for Worship

Near the end of his sabbatical year Bill felt led to write up a talk which he had given many, many times at Pendle Hill, "The Four Doors to Meeting for Worship." He set aside half a day each day until it was finished. Looking back, he comments, "It worked." It did not take long to complete the pamphlet because he had honed this topic for many years. In a little over two weeks time he had a first draft.

This pamphlet has been well received by Quaker meetings. It is particularly helpful for new attenders who may feel adrift sitting in the silence of meeting for worship. It has been equally well received by seasoned Friends.

For Bill, a doorway provides an "anchor;" a reminder to remember God. He says, "Going through that door is always a time of prayerful awareness, not a verbal prayer, but the door is a symbol of entering into a new state of consciousness, a new state of being, a new adventure."

Of the four doors discussed in his pamphlet, Bill particularly likes the "door before." This is the idea that one dips into the stream of living water many times a day and thus prepares oneself for meeting for worship on First day. Bill says, "I continue to learn about that. I think I will as long as I live." Brother Lawrence called it "Practicing the Presence." Bill says, "I don't think I will ever be a Brother Lawrence who seemed to be in that state all the time, but I love to keep working at it."

The other part of his pamphlet which Bill likes is in the part about the "door within." He talks about times when he was not able to give vocal ministry in meeting. It was then he discovered there was a deeper level of ministry than he had previously understood, the level of silent radiation. Bill says, "A person ministers to the people around one without words, simply radiates the kind of energy which is not one's own but is flowing through one. I suddenly realized with a great shock of humility that my gift in vocal ministry often depended very often upon the very inconspicuous men and women who never spoke, who did not even know they were doing this."

When working on a project like writing a pamphlet or a talk, Bill approaches his desk as he would an altar. He says:

Whenever I would come to the desk I would seek to be in a worshipful, obedient state as one would when going before the altar in a high Catholic Church. When I was preparing for my course on prayer at Pendle Hill, I felt so unprepared and unworthy that months before I taught the course, when preparing for it, whenever I went to my desk to work on it, I would take off my shoes. My desk became a sacred place where a lot of my significant work took place.

Bill says, "I tend to get to writing something when there is a deadline. Somebody asks me to give a talk, and I say, 'Yes, I could do that.' Then it comes forth in a talk."
He explains:

Temperamentally I am the kind of a person who tends to do what is before me. So my own projects, if I'm not careful, tend to get put aside if there is some need that is really clear that I need to pay attention to. Part of my discernment process is to ask, 'Am I needed?' 'Am I the best person in this situation?' When I see I have something to offer and I don't see anyone else who can offer it, I step in.

Fran

For several years prior to the sabbath year, Fran had been suffering from chronic fatigue. She had a bout of pneumonia in 1986, followed by a very slow recovery of her energy. For a time following the pneumonia, while at Pendle Hill, she spent her days lying on a sofa. It was impossible for her to take walks. In spite of her depleted energy, she was able to complete a course at Shalem Institute for Spiritual Direction and coordinated the retreat program for Pendle Hill.

In contrast to the intensity of Pendle Hill life, a sabbath year at home in Barnesville looked attractive to her. She says, "I envisioned a quieter, more contemplative, less people-intensive time, nourishing on a deep level in a way different from Pendle Hill."

The first thing Fran did not foresee was that she would still be suffering from chronic fatigue. Fortunately, early on in the Sabbath year, Fran found a homeopathic woman doctor in Pittsburgh who diagnosed her condition as Epstein-Barr virus and gave suggestions of remedial steps to take. This included medication, diet, and exercise. By February of the sabbath year, Fran's health condition was much improved. Fran was able to move into a more regular work schedule.

The main focus of her work that year was research for a projected book on the life of her father as an example of Quaker character. The idea for this project had come to her as a leading some years before.

The Nudge

Fran recalls vividly the moment in which she first became aware of a nudge to write about her father. It was at a Friends workshop on "Spiritual Gifts" in 1983. She recalls:

> At one point in the workshop we were asked to draw ourselves doing something we felt drawn to do. I drew myself writing about my father. It felt kind of unreal, but that is what came to me.

Fran's father had died in the fall of 1982 at the age of 95. His life span stretched almost a century, from covered wagon days until the nuclear age. She says, "His life had been a unique one, one that is remarkable in my mind for the persistence of his attempt to live out faithfully his faith as he understood it. He had an independent turn of mind with which he interpreted and lived out his faith. So I began to dream of writing something about his life."

Part of the appeal of writing about her parents was that they were strong examples of how Conservative Friends lived their lives. Fran's parents were what is called "plain Friends." This term referred to their simplicity of lifestyle, their honesty and integrity, the careful way they used words to express what they knew to be true, and their use of plain dress. Fran's father wore a black hat with uncreased crown. As a young man he had the lapels removed from his suit coat, but in later years he gave up wearing a suit in favor of fresh clean work clothes for going to meeting. Her mother's dresses were simply cut and unadorned, worn with black stockings and shoes. She rarely got out her bonnet, finding a scarf or beret simpler.

Unexpected Treasure

While Fran had contemplated writing about her father while she was at Pendle Hill, she did not find time there to do it. She noticed that the idea just did not go away. Fran sees this as one characteristic of a true leading. She says, "One part of clearness was the persistence with which this stayed in my mind over several years and continued to be something that carried a lot of energy with it."

It was the finding of an unexpected treasure that moved her forward. When Fran's mother moved, in 1984, from the family home in northern Ohio to a retirement home in Barnesville, Ohio, Fran and Bill had the task of cleaning out the family home. One day Fran was sitting on the south steps of the house when Bill brought her an old cardboard box he had found in the closed-in front porch. Fran recalls that by this time Bill was eager to find things to throw out.

Bill asked, "Shall I throw this out?" The box was full of old letters. Fran looked at one of the letters and told Bill, "No."

Fran says, "These were my parents' courtship letters which I did not know existed. I had asked Mother whether she had the letters. She was around ninety and a little vague and replied, "Oh, I don't know . . . probably not."

This courtship spanned sixteen months from when Fran's parents first met until shortly before marriage. Fran's mother, Mary, lived in Salem, Ohio, and Fran's father, Sheldon, lived in Springvalle, Iowa. The couple only saw each other twice during this time. Some of the letters were as long as twelve or even twenty pages. When the whole lot was transcribed it filled 906 double-spaced pages.

As Fran read some of the letters she grew excited. What moved her most was the gentleness and thoroughness with which her parents wrote to each other. She says, "They shared what was going on in their families, their neighborhoods, and in the meeting family. They were careful to share with one another their thoughts and feelings about basically everything important to them in life, starting with religion. Before long, each reported to the other, as near as they could think, all their characteristic faults so that in the event they were married there would be no unpleasant surprises."

Fran did not consider herself to be a writer. She had never written a book. But she began to think more and more about such a project. She took a course in story telling which heightened her conviction of the importance of telling our stories. She was aware of the importance story telling has played in carrying on the traditions and testimonies of Quakerism. She says, "Many groups find their identity through such things as creeds. Quakers, in avoiding creeds, have to depend upon stories of personal experiences." Fran knew her parents' story could be a significant piece of the history showing the way of life of Conservative Friends in the 1920s.

Research

In order to get started on this project during her sabbath year, Fran had to give it a big priority. Fran says, "My biggest difficulty was simply finding the time, in the context of my life, to work my project in among other things that seems equally a part of what my life is about." She says, "The first significant way of working it out was making this project the centerpiece of that year's leave of absence. That really got it off the ground."

In the fall of the sabbath year, Fran began by reading oral history and other people's writings about their parents. She realized that significant material would need to come from interviews with family members and friends. In January Bill and Fran took a trip south, shaped around interviews with some of the oldest of these family members and friends. They visited a 95-year-old man who had known Fran's father as young conscientious objector during World War I.

By the end of the winter of the sabbath year, Fran had read through the complete set of courtship letters. She says, "I found these interesting enough that they altered the shape of my project. My mother began to take a larger place in my vision of what I would like to write. I began to feel the letters should tell a large part of the story." Fran could see that her parents' story could illustrate the lifestyle and values of Conservative Friends of that era. She says, "They were good candidates because of their extraordinary commitment to live their faith."

Discernment

Even during a "sabbath year," it was not easy for Fran to make time for her research and writing project. Fran points out that living in rural Ohio among Conservative Friends puts certain expectations on them. She says, "In this setting it is not easy to say that I am going to take half of every day writing. There is not the expectation that this is the kind of thing that people will be about. It is harder to take time, to reserve time for writing or quiet time or taking retreats or whatever."

At one point, some time later, Fran was feeling the need to explain to people in her meeting that she needed to reserve regular time to work on this book. She invited several members of her meeting community to come to a clearness committee. She wrote up a page of explanation about her book project, putting forth her leading in as convincing a way as she could. The small group of Conservative Friends sat in worship together while she asked them to consider her leading to do this work. Did they feel it was important for her to do it? Whether or not they fully understood it, these Friends were willing to accept that it was in right order for Fran to follow her leading. This helped, at least for a time. People would sometimes ask her after meeting how the writing was coming.

Fran had to deal with the doubts that beset many writers. Questions would come up in her mind: "Is anybody interested?" "Can I do it?" "Who am I to have the nerve to do this?" Yet this has been offset by an internal sense of rightness. She continues to have a sense of excitement when she gets into this project. "My mind gets going," she says. "My fingers start itching."

The research on her parents was not the only focus for her work during the sabbath year. One invitation which Fran accepted was to travel, as an elder, with a recorded minister from Fran's meeting, on a visit to Iowa Yearly Meeting. The two women carried a minute from their home meeting, attended Yearly Meeting, and made several home visits in which they had opportunities for worship with local families.

Fran says:

> This was my first experience of the traditional Friends' model of traveling, in the role of elder, with a minister. The elder is the companion who is encourager, helper in discernment, and assistant with practical arrangements.

This travel was in line with Fran's calling to teach spiritual nurture through "A School of the Spirit," a fledgling program at that time.

At the end of the sabbath year, Fran wrote:

> As I look back on the year, the most significant thing about it seems to be the way, full of mystery and full of creation, in which God is able to take our dreams, our intention, and the willingness of our commitment, and to do with them things we could not have imagined. I reflect on how God uses the thoughts we can think, and the things we are able to envision, to put us in place for the work we could not have foreseen.

Fruits of the Sabbatical Year

Both Bill and Fran came back from their sabbath year refreshed. Both of them began the year with low energy, but by the end of the year both had regained their health, strength, and energy. During the year away, they had worked on writing projects, Bill producing a pamphlet and Fran making progress on a book. They found ways to be of service to their Yearly Meeting and to Olney School. The opportunity to be home living among Conservative Friends regrounded them in their own religious tradition, so that they could better continue their role as interpreters between branches of Friends. Perhaps the best part of the sabbath year was that they had a chance to sink into the feeling of spaciousness, both inner and outer, so that they could learn to dwell more fully in the Presence of the Lord.

III. THE CALL

Lucy McIver

Lucy McIver

*There is in each of us a deep-flowing River.
Some call it the Tao or Lifesource, others the
Indwelling Spirit, still others call it simply
Energy. Our life rests upon It; we are carried
and cradled by It, as the child by its Mother.*

Pendle Hill Pamphlet # 304
Mind What Stirs In Your Heart
—Teresina Havens

*L*ucy McIver welcomes me into her home in Eugene, Oregon for a mid-April interview. She shows me around her garden with her "greenhouse" put together with discarded windows, her tiny tomato plants still in the starter boxes soaking up the sun, the lime green early lettuce in a sheltered spot, and deep purple iris in bloom. We sit on the newly constructed redwood deck and enjoy the warmth of the spring day.

Lucy is a small woman, just five feet tall. She is in her late fifties. Many of her art works decorate this home which she shares with her partner. In one room is Lucy's loom with which she makes place mats and shawls. As we settle down in the living room, we are surrounded by three of Lucy's "dream catchers," beautiful mandalas made of wood and yarn. Lucy uses this space for her clients who come for therapy sessions.

Lucy's story illustrates receiving a spiritual call in a very dramatic way from a woman who is to become her mentor. From that moment on Lucy is led on a journey which winds around many bends. In Cry Pain, Cry Hope (p.82), Elizabeth O'Connor writes about such journeys:

> Call asks that we set out from a place that is familiar and relatively secure for a destination that can be only dimly perceived, and that we cannot be at all certain of reaching, so many are the obstacles that will loom along the way. One of the ways to test the authenticity of call is to determine whether it requires a journey. This journey is not necessarily geographic although, as in the case of Abraham and Moses, it is not at all unusual for it to involved leaving one's work and home. Whether or not the call includes an outward journey, it always requires an inward one. We need to be delivered from all that binds us and keeps the real self from breaking into music and becoming joy to the world.

O'Connor emphasizes that when we feel God's call, we feel it deep within. She says:

> The first stretch of the inward journey is touching in some vital way our own deepest feelings. To see visions or to hear call without being faithful to one's most ardent yearnings is utterly impossible. Our strongest feelings revolve around our wants and desires, and we have been taught since our first summer to give these only slight attention, so that when we think about drawing close to our real longings we have feelings of guilt and shame. It is as though our deepest wishes were unworthy and, if pursued, could get us into all kinds of trouble and at the very least cause us to feel or be called selfish. The opposite, of course, is true.

Lucy sits quietly, her white hair plaited into a single braid, her eyes shut. We take some time in silent worship to ground the interview under the direction of God. When Lucy begins to speak, her voice is almost a whisper, her expression intense, for the story Lucy is to tell me took her on a long journey, fulfilled her deepest longings, and changed her life forever.

Meeting Teresina

Meeting Teresina Havens was a life-changing event for Lucy. Lucy was fifty-three years old. She had been divorced from her husband a year earlier. Their four children were grown by then. She had worshipped with Quakers for twelve years and had joined Eugene Friends Meeting. At that time she was living in her own home and renting a room to a friend. Lucy was working as director of a community fitness center and swimming pool in town.

Lucy says, "I had sought out Teresina at Quarterly Meeting after I had read a rough copy of her pamphlet, *Mind What*

Stirs in your Heart. The pamphlet was about incorporating movement into Friends' times of worship. I wanted to know more about that." Innocent enough? Lucy simply wanted to know more about a pamphlet she had read.

Lucy remembers the encounter vividly: Teresina was 83 years old and conscious of the need to slow down. Lucy recalls, "We sat watching a beautiful sunset over a lake, talking about the value of moving our bodies, dance, and touching the Spirit through these gifts. I told her I had danced all my life but that a few years ago I felt that I had done everything in dance that I was being told to do and that it was time for me to move on to something else."

Then came the jolt. "Teresina looked at me very intensely and said, "No, there's much more for you to do in dance." Those words struck home. Lucy explains, "Teresina was very charismatic, very spiritual, and she looked right into my heart, and I knew she was right. I think this was a pivotal point."

Background

In order to explain her response to Teresina's call, Lucy told me about how dancing became significant in her childhood. Long before Lucy's birth, her mother birthed a still-born baby boy. Lucy's sister was born a year after, and Lucy was born ten years after her sister. Lucy suffered from the knowledge that her mother did not want her. Years later, as an adult, Lucy recovered flashback memories of being in her crib and knowing she was not wanted. "I could see and feel my mother tying me into the crib. I could see the bars of the crib and I could not move. I remember feeling the darkness entering me, penetrating me, and feeling desperately alone." Lucy told her sister about this and her sister confirmed, "I remember her standing over the crib screaming at you; I was so afraid that I would go and hide under my bed because I didn't want her to scream at me."

When Lucy was one year old, her father's parents came to live with the family. Lucy says, "I believe they must have come because my father didn't know what to do. Mother was angry and abusing the children." After that her mother worked outside the home in the small appliance business her father ran. Lucy was cared for by her loving grandmother, who became the homemaker for the family. She says, "I can remember my grandmother holding me for the first time; I can visualize her face and feel her arms around me as she was rocking me and saying, 'You're safe now; you're safe. It's okay.'" Lucy says, "Frequently it was just Grandmother and me at home. I remember putting on Chopin or Tchaikovsky and just dancing wildly in the living room." Lucy understood, even as a child, that to dance and perform was her role in the family.

Lucy deeply appreciates her grandmother.

> My Grandmother gave me the greatest gift that any child can receive. She was my friend. She gave me the feeling that she really enjoyed my company, valued me as a person. That was a tremendous gift to me.

Lucy's paternal grandfather is Native American, from the Choctaw tribe. When Lucy was a youngster, her grandfather used to take her out in a small boat very early in the mornings to hunt for frogs. Frogs legs were part of the family diet. Her grandfather taught her to sit very still, to listen, and to attune herself to a big bull frog sitting on the river bank. Her grandfather told her she must let her spirit enter into the frog's and the frog's spirit enter into hers before it was time to pick the frog up gently and place him in the box on the side of the boat. Her grandfather taught her to attune herself to all the creatures of the natural world. This ability is an essential part of how Lucy relates to the world today.

After Lucy grew up, married, and began to have children, she was too busy to spend much time dancing. She and her husband raised four children in a log cabin in Idaho. Lucy washed diapers with a wringer washer every day and hung them to dry on a line over the wood stove in winter. Lucy was thoroughly involved with nurturing her young children, including nursing them as babies. The fourth child was adopted at age six weeks while Lucy was still nursing her third child. Lucy nursed two babies for a time. "I've always been very attuned to natural processes," she comments.

Another of Lucy's loves was nurturing her garden, her flowers, and her vegetables. This has been a life-long passion.

Gradually, over the years, Lucy and her husband grew apart. Lucy became depressed. She says, "I remember one morning sitting in my living room. My husband was sitting in his chair talking away about who knows what. I looked at him and, for the first time, verbalized inwardly to myself, 'I really don't love this man any more.'" Lucy understood that she and her husband had grown in different directions. Now, without the children to keep them together, there was not much left between." Lucy says, "The discernment was very profound." Lucy comments that every turning point in her life has become crystal clear for her long in advance of acting on the knowing.

Teresina's Call

It was only a year after the divorce that Lucy met Teresina. Teresina was 83 years old, a very strong-minded, outspoken Quaker woman, a former college professor. Teresina and her husband had started and directed a retreat center in New England. Teresina loved to move to music and to inspirational poems. She was in the period of life in which she wanted to pass on her gifts to others. Lucy was ready to receive. She says that she felt like she had been in a "cocoon" state since her divorce. "I went into the cocoon where my chrysalis was spun. I discovered this great need inside of me to be silent, to listen, like I did when I was a child."

Meeting Teresina was a turning point, not only for Lucy but also for Teresina. From that moment on, the lives of these two women were linked. Lucy recalls how the two of them went out on the lawn in the dusk. It was a clear night and the stars were coming out. Teresina sang the hymn, "For the Beauty of the Earth," and the two women danced together. "It was a special moment," says Lucy.

Lucy's body expressed what was happening. Lucy says, "I remember feeling a weight inside of me. It was like something was happening, and I was frightened. The something was so much bigger than myself that I could not understand it. My body didn't even want to move, I felt so shy. It was like being so exposed."

She remembers Teresina trying to encourage her by saying, "You just need some warm-ups. Why don't you come and spend a weekend with us on Thanksgiving? We'll spend all day in the meetinghouse dancing and I'll show you what you need to do." Lucy accepted.

Dancing with Teresina

Thanksgiving weekend in Portland, Lucy joined Teresina and her husband, Joe, also a long-time Quaker. Joe, in his seventies, was eleven years younger than Teresina. Lucy recalls, "All day Friday we were at the meetinghouse. Teresina had brought some music, but also she had brought some quotes of early Friends, George Fox and John Woolman. That was the beginning of learning how to use scripture or sacred writing as a motivation for movement.

"I remember there was a quote about anointing with sacred oil. Teresina had brought an old plastic bottle of corn oil. It was so funny, this common, partially-melted plastic bottle that had been sitting in her kitchen for a year or two.

You know how gummy oil bottles get. We were using it as a sacred object in order to anoint and it was wonderful. She never put oil on my head, but she blessed my head with her hand and we blessed each other. It was a symbolic gesture. Then she sat me down and blessed my feet, massaging them. It was like being given something very great."

Lucy recalls how her shyness fell away and she began to bond with Teresina. Another dancer, a mutual friend, Betsy Kenworthy, joined them and the three women spent the afternoon dancing and sharing. Teresina spoke about being at the age when one must give up one's burdens and suggested that they dance this experience.

Lucy recalls, "She took her little neck scarf and tied it around her head as if she had the mumps. Then she tucked her date book into the scarf. The date book symbolized all her obligations. As her witness, I went up to her and held out my hands to see if she wanted to give it to me. She clung to it and brought it to her chest and sighed and sighed. You could tell she was just in great labor over this. When we finished dancing we sat in a worshipful mode and shared.

Says Lucy, "Teresina said that there were so many burdens and she had to finish them. She had to start letting go and could not take on new things. She talked to me about working with her at Friends General Conference and co-facilitating the workshop she was already committed to lead. I agreed."

Again Lucy had little conscious idea of where that commitment might lead. Yet on some subconscious level, Lucy must have known because she noticed a shift in her own behavior. Lucy remembers sitting with Teresina and Joe that evening, "talking and blabbering, telling my whole life story to these people that I didn't even know." Thinking back on it, Lucy comments, "I'm a fairly quiet person. It was the strangest thing to look back on."

Saturday morning it was raining and Joe wanted some time alone. Teresina suggested that she and Lucy go to the

Japanese gardens in Portland. Lucy recalls, "Teresina and I walked along with this big umbrella in silence through the Japanese Gardens. I remember sitting in one of the little shelters and listening to all the sounds of water, the rain coming, the little stream, the little fountain, water would trickle and gather and then be released. We sat. I felt aware of so much, being in Teresina's presence."

Lucy relates, "When we came home, Teresina said to Joe, 'Lucy's really in tune with nature. She's really open.' We had said very little, but there was a communication going between us. I didn't understand what was happening, but I knew it was happening."

Looking back, Lucy comments, "I think I was being opened up by God at that point, that Teresina was a channel for this to come through. She was very sensitive because of where she was in her life. " Lucy says, "We began the day lighting a candle and listening to music or moving a little bit. It just kindled in me all that I had not done since I was a child, that freedom to just be alone and move to music, or just dance out among the trees, or sit and watch a flower for a long time, and be attuned to nature. I was feeling the energies from the plants and trees. I began to somehow communicate with birds and wildlife again, which I had done as a child but had forgotten about."

Lucy, Joe, and Teresina made plans for a weekend in Eugene the end of January. Joe would help to start an economics interest group at Eugene Friends Meeting. Teresina would do an afternoon sharing of movement and worship.

The Challenge

In mid-January Joe called Lucy to say that Teresina had been diagnosed with congestive heart failure. She was refusing by-pass surgery. Joe said he would come to Eugene Friends Meeting to lead the workshop but Teresina would not be able to come. Lucy says:

Teresina got on the phone and asked me at that time if I would do the Friends General Conference workshop for her. I was in denial. I could not believe she was going to go so quickly. It was my fear that I couldn't do the workshop at Friends General Conference at all. I said I had to have time to think about it.

When Joe came to Eugene in early February, he encouraged me to lead the movement and worship sharing that Teresina was scheduled to do at the meetinghouse.

Lucy comments:

That was the beginning; I picked several exercises from Teresina's pamphlet and used those. It was scary . . . new ground for me.

The next day Joe and Lucy took a long walk. Joe told her, "Teresina needs to know your answer, if you are going to lead the workshop at Friends General Conference. She needs to talk to you. I think you should come up to Portland soon."

Lucy hesitated, telling Joe, "It's so new to me. It is scary to think of leading workshops for Teresina." Lucy was in a state of disbelief and full of fear. She told Joe, "I can hardly believe she is dying this quickly." Thinking back on it, Lucy comments, "Once again I denied."

On Tuesday, February 11, Joe called Lucy, begging, "Lucy, Teresina's time is getting short, you need to come to Portland." This time Lucy said she would talk with her supervisor and see if she could get off work, but she added, "I won't promise." Lucy hung up the phone. She never did talk with her supervisor. She relates, with chagrin, "A third time I was in denial. I was so frightened."

On Thursday, February 13, Lucy received "this immense urge to call her." When Lucy telephoned, however, she was told that Teresina was too weak to come to the phone. Lucy hung up, wondering if her response had come too late. But all day long she was conscious that somehow she had to speak to Teresina. Lucy remembers, "By that evening this burning inside of me was about ready to explode."

Lucy telephoned again. This time Teresina's son answered and rigged up the phone so she could talk. Teresina's voice was very weak as she told Lucy, "I want you, Carla de Sota, and Betsy Kenworthy to dance my rites of passage on Sunday. It's all arranged. Will you come up on Sunday whether I'm here or not?" Lucy agreed. Then came the question, "Will you do the workshop at FGC?" Lucy says:

> I heard my voice talking, somewhere far away, 'Yes, Teresina, I will do it.' I had no clue what that meant. I was shaking all over

Teresina said, "That's my last burden. It's a great relief, a great gift. Now let me ask you, Will you carry on my work?" Again Lucy heard herself say, "Yes." Lucy began shaking and did not stop for many days.

The die was cast. From deep within Lucy, some part of herself, a part she hardly even recognized, had stepped forward and said, "Yes." Lucy seemed to feel it was not her conscious self that made that decision. The voice came from deep within and seemed to be not under her own control.

A door had opened, and Lucy had stepped through it. Lucy reports that she couldn't understand what was happening at the time. Yet Lucy's body expressed what she must have known on a deep cellular level. "The tears kept coming," she says. "It was very powerful."

Next morning, Friday, February fourteenth, Lucy got up and started moving in her living room. She reports, "I knew I had to move. I couldn't breathe unless I was moving." Teresina's life on earth ended that afternoon, Valentine's Day, fitting for a woman who was so loved.

That evening Lucy felt drawn to join a group of Friends who were doing dances at the meetinghouse. She says, "I knew I had to be in the meeting room, and I knew I had to be dancing. I felt that somehow that circle of Friends could contain me and offer me some safety."

Once again, when she needed support and a safe container, Lucy sought the worship room of her meetinghouse. This space seemed to be a place that centered her, a place in which she felt the love and comfort of God and her community of Friends.

Next morning Lucy received the news from Betsy, "She's gone." Betsy had been with Teresina when she passed over. Betsy described how Teresina had quietly gone into herself and let go. Although Teresina stopped being responsive to questions, she seemed to be conscious right up to the last.

Dancing the Rites of Passage

On Sunday, two days later, Betsy, Carla, and Lucy danced the rites of passage. Before people arrived, Lucy sat in the sun and allowed herself to center. She remembers thinking in her mind, "Why am I here? What is this? I really don't know these people and yet I know them so well." Her logical mind was wrestling with the surrender that had been called for and with all that was happening. She comments, looking back, "It had happened so quickly!"

When friends and family had gathered, the dance began. Lucy describes how the three of them arranged Teresina's photograph in some cedar boughs with the Buddha and other mementos people had brought. One of them read a quotation Teresina had liked by a seventeenth-century Friend, Richard Hubberthorne.

> This night or tomorrow night I shall depart hence.
> Do not seek to hold me for it is too straight for me,
> and out of this straightness I must go for I am wound
> into largeness.

"I remember not wanting to turn away from the altar," says Lucy. "We pulled her spirit away from the altar and released it out over the hills on the far side of the Colombia

River. At the end we all gathered around Joe and gently rocked him."

Preparation

The next stage was preparation for the workshop. Lucy was still working at the swimming pool, but she carved out time for her interior work as well. She says:

> If I was to do a Friends General Conference work-shop, I knew I couldn't just walk in the door and do the workshop. I had to understand what was happening to me.

Again Lucy turned to her meeting room space. She got a key to the meetinghouse and went over there at 5:30 every morning. She started with rereading Teresina's pamphlet exercises from *Mind What Stirs in the Heart*. "I did every one of those exercises," she says.

The pamphlet includes exercises based on Quaker quotes. Sometimes she would do one for several days until the meaning would come to her. Lucy had faith that if Teresina had heard something in John Woolman's words, there must be something sacred there. "I went on in faith and worked with each passage until I began to sense the life in those words." Lucy grew to understand what Teresina had meant by "carry on my work." Lucy was to take Teresina's work into herself and make it hers, in her own way. From her journal entries written during those morning sessions, Lucy developed the workshop for the Friends General Conference Gathering.

Lucy says this morning spiritual practice had a strong effect on her. She says:

> I came in communication with the spirit within me, in intimacy. Moments of ecstasy often overcame me. My concentration, my ability to center and listen within became acute. I was clearly being led by the

Spirit rather than my own ego. My body changed. I became stronger, my life richer, more meaningful.

This was a time of preparation. Preparation time is essential when one is beginning to follow a leading. When Jesus began his ministry, he went off into the desert for forty days. That was for him a time of wrestling with demonic forces and connecting with God the Father. He was grounding himself in that connection, preparing for what was to come.

When an acorn is cracked open and a sapling begins to grow, the preliminary growth takes place underground. The first tiny roots and the first small signs of a stalk emerge in the dark womb of the earth. So the interior work of preparation for spiritual ministry occurs deep inside the soul. God's work may be in process within a person although we cannot see anything happening.

Lucy made space for her internal work by setting aside the early morning time for God's work. She was working full time at the swimming pool, yet she carved out a daily chunk of time and chose a quiet location where she would not be disturbed. Lucy was opening herself to the work of the Spirit. She was giving herself over to be guided, to be molded.

At Friends General Conference, Lucy's workshop was intense—daily three-hour sessions for a week. Participants learned to move from a worshipful mode, expressing their deepest inward feelings, and they learned to witness to the movements of others. Leading this workshop was affirming for Lucy. "I felt bonded in spirit with the people in my workshop on a level I'd never known as a teacher," she says. "I knew that I would continue in this work."

At the end of the Conference, Lucy knew she had only scratched the surface of the work to which she felt led. She returned home to continue her daily meditations. She says, "I felt it necessary to work alone more deeply to find the depths of spirit required in my leadership."

In August Lucy heard that Marylhurst College in Portland, Oregon, had just started a certification course in Dance/ Movement Therapy. Lucy felt a pull to enroll but wondered how could she pay for it. She continued to work at the fitness center at the same time as she continued her morning movement and meditation in the meetinghouse.

Encounters with Forces of Darkness

Lucy reports:

> As the fall progressed, the complexion of my morning meditations took a different path. I became concerned. I was having feelings of terror, of being terrorized. I did not know what these all meant. I had started to uncover these childhood memories and I knew that darkness or violence had been a part of my life. Sometimes, as I moved in the meetinghouse, I experienced this tremendous energy within me, driving my movement. I did not feel it was evil but I could feel its power. Often times as I was moving and working with memories, the energy would propel me in ways my body wouldn't normally have moved. I had a great respect for this energy, but I did not have a name for it.

Lucy spoke to Joe Havens about this. Joe suggested she consult with Janet Adler, a mutual friend who is a movement therapist and teacher. Janet gave Lucy guidelines for safety. Janet validated the idea that these experiences were a sign of a deep level of spiritual maturity. Lucy recalls, "Janet said I must continue this work, not turn away from it in fear."

Lucy grew to understand it in this way:

> The months of moving, listening, and concentration had opened me to all the pain I had experienced as an abused child—the pain that I had buried at a

cellular level to survive. This pain has opened me to a new mystical depth in communication with others and the Spirit.

It was at this time that Lucy recovered memories of the abuse she suffered from her mother as a very young child. Although the recovery of memories was very frightening, Lucy knew she must face her fears.

In the midst of all this inner work, Lucy was finding it more and more difficult to do the practical work of managing the pool. Again she consulted with Joe. He suggested taking a retreat. Lucy decided upon an all-night vigil, seeking divine assurance for her call to movement therapy. She chose the meetinghouse where she felt spiritually protected. She took the precaution of telling people her plans and arranged for a friend to come in the early morning hours.

Lucy explains that it is hard to put into words what happened. Because this experience was a turning point for her life she tried to describe it as best she could. She says some parts of it are hard to explain—she still does not understand it all. She relates:

> On November 10, 1992, I entered the meeting room at 10:00 p.m. There I spent the night in meditation, dancing, letting music and Spirit lead me wherever. I completely submitted myself. I could feel this energy beginning to come up. At one point I remember a vision of an arched doorway, looking through to a light on the other side, feeling like I needed to move into that Light. I remember kneeling there and wanting desperately to move into that Light and somehow not having the energy within me to do that. I felt that if I got across, it would be warm, but I couldn't step through. I remember turning away from this vision and moving in the darkness and a voice coming that said, "You must go down to the floor."

> Before I could kneel and get my body on the floor, I felt an energy just push me, and I fell with great force. I hit my head on the floor. I was stunned; I just lay there for a long time.

Lucy was frightened. She remembers a putrid smell. She sobbed and shook until her friend came. Her friend held her for a long time until her feelings subsided. It was at this time, in her state of complete physical exhaustion, that Lucy received the inner assurance she had been seeking. She was to become a movement therapist. The message that came to her was this:

> I had all the tools within me to do the work, and, most important, the way would open for me to go back to school to prepare myself for this work.

This was the turning point. Lucy felt that her complete submission and recognition of the darkness had spiritually led her "through the arch" into the light. This experience proved to her the power of movement as a healing tool. But she knew that she needed to learn much more about movement and how to structure it safely as a therapeutic tool. She began to study Authentic Movement with Janet Adler, who became Lucy's spiritual director as well.

Back to School

The profound experiences that Lucy was having were nudging her. She made the decision to leave her job and move to Portland where she could enroll in the master's degree program in Dance/Movement Therapy at Marylhurst College. Joe offered her space in his home in Portland. She received a grant from the Lyman Fund to help pay tuition costs. Lucy was the first student to be accepted into the new program. Was it just a lucky coincidence that a degree program opened up at precisely the time Lucy needed one, in the city where Joe lived and could offer her a place to stay? Or was this synchronicity—sometimes defined as "a coincidence in which God chooses to remain anonymous"?

Lucy continued to practice her morning meditations and movement in prayer. She wrote:

> I have grown in relationship with God. The more I come to be independent within myself, the more dependent I become on divine guidance. Through meditation and prayer, I am coming to see myself more clearly as a simple extension of God. I feel that all life is continuous, that each soul is a segment of all, that I am you, you are me, we are God. My spiritual work is to accept my individuality and strengthen the connection between my inner being, others, and God.

Lucy had grown in ways she had never imagined possible before she met Teresina. In April, she wrote:

> The more deeply I follow this path, the more I lose myself—Lucy. As I reflect back on this last year, I don't even recognize the woman I knew. Truly I have been blessed, guided by angels towards work that is to be done.

The Journey Continues

Lucy's journey began with a "Yes" to Teresina's request, "Will you carry on my work?" This charge, fully lived into, became the larger charge from God, "Will you carry on My Work?" The manifestation of God's intention through Lucy continues to develop as the leading shifts. Lucy now works as a therapist, broadening the scope of her work from movement therapy to many expressive art therapy modalities.

She comments:

> The years of authentic movement in my own practice have taught me to have an inner witness that is

objective so I can journey (with my clients) into their inner depths, but my inner witness knows when it is too deep and when to pull them back up. That is the intuitive process that goes on all the time as I practice. I am discovering I can only see to go into it with prayer. I ask for guidance. I readily admit that I am totally incapable of doing this work and that I can only do it with guidance, that I have no answers. I surrender completely to the process.

Lucy's journey of responding to God's call has been one of surrender. She comments:

I don't know about other people's leadings but it seems to me as if God always asks me to do preposterous things, expecting that I just do it. But then God always provides the people to help. I have a "knowing" of the work God wants me to do, even though there are feelings of being incapable for the task. But I must plunge forward, and that in itself feels wonderful.

IV. PRAYER AND CONTEMPLATION

Kathryn Damiano

Kathryn Damiano

*Once you are joined to the Lord, you become
as omnipresent as (he) is. Instead of offering
assistance in one particular place, doctor, nurse,
or priest, on the power of the cross you have
the ability to be everywhere at once.*

St. Teresa Benedicta of the Cross, OCD
The Flame, *Newsletter of the Association
of Contemplative Sisters, Fall 1998*

*K*athryn Damiano sits quietly in the Quaker meeting room, a lone figure absorbed in prayer. Her dark hair is tied back in a bun. She is wearing a simple purple blouse, flowered skirt, white sandals. Her gold-rimmed glasses reflect the light. Kathryn is doing what she feels called to do . . . praying.

This is her ministry, living and working within the over-all scope of a life centered in prayer. She just turned fifty this year and is working as a spiritual director at a Quaker cen-ter for study and contemplation. This morning she has come early to meet in my room for an interview.

Kathryn works as a spiritual director, praying for and with people. When people are nudged by the Spirit, they usually feel the need for deeper prayer. They often need someone to pray with them in order to know how to respond. God's ways are not human ways and God's leadings often go against the cultural mainstream. The harder it is to walk the path, the stronger must grow the roots. Just as the roots of a tree spread out beneath the surface to support the branches overhead, so a leading requires extensive prayer to support its weight as it grows and branches out.

At the beginning stages this may mean a period of morning prayer. As one develops in a life of faith, one learns to take everything to God in prayer. In time this prayer life may grow into practicing the presence of God throughout the day. As the person grows in trust, leaning on those everlasting arms, this relationship with God sets the tone for whatever goes on in the small daily interactions of one's life.

Kathryn is a contemplative. Sandra Cronk who worked closely with Kathryn described contemplation in **Dark Night Journey** *(p. 57):*

> *Deeper knowing (i.e., unknowing or loving) is what the Christian tradition has called contemplation. It is a way of prayer, but it might better be understood*

as a whole way of being. . . . The Christian heritage customarily defines contemplation in distinction to meditation as a style of prayer. Meditation is the systematic reflection on an idea, biblical verse, an image (e.g., the cross), or a question. . . . Contemplation describes a different kind of prayer, the pure gift of being with God. In this prayer, systematic exploration of a theme becomes impossible. Even devotional reading seems useless. . . . The analytical faculties which were used so richly in meditation are now silent. They can force no meaning or insights from what they read or think about. Because of the exterior stripping process, the old ways of experiencing God's gifts in the world have disappeared. In this situation it may no longer be possible to "know about" God, but it is possible to enter a new and deeper relationship with God.

Kathryn Damiano is well immersed in a life of prayer and contemplation. Her story illustrates how a person with such a prayer life responds in the midst of anxious moments and practical difficulties.

Kathryn describes prayer in this way:

The image of a flowing river comes to me. We tap into the prayer that is already happening. That is where leadings come from. One has to be in a centered place over time and glean out the distractions to get to the pure living water and to dip into that. It is not even a new idea. It is what God has spoken into the world already, and we are just tapping into it. That is where the leading begins.

And then there is a quickening, and a continuing birth as it takes different forms and nuances. I've never been pregnant with a baby, but I have been pregnant with the Spirit. You know there is life, but

> *you don't know what you are going to give birth to. You worry as would a pregnant woman: "Will it be deformed? Will I be able to care for it? Will I be able to follow through? How will it change my life?"There's nothing you can do. It is beyond your control. It is in God's hands, in God's plan, in God's time.*

Kathryn spoke about being in that place during the previous year when she was unemployed and waiting to find the job God wanted her to take.

"The contemplative journey is not for everybody," she says:

> *The discernment shifts. The leadings are not so clear anymore. They are not: "Do this" or "Take on this project." It is "Show up where you are asked and be faithful," not even knowing, sometimes, what faithfulness means. So on one level it doesn't get clearer, but the anchor is there, stronger.*

A few years ago Kathryn and her friend Sandra Cronk were led to pray together on a regular basis. Out of this ministry of prayer came the seed for a ministry of learning. Other people joined with them to develop courses in spirituality, forming the organization, "A Ministry of Prayer and Learning devoted to the School of the Spirit," commonly shortened to "The School of the Spirit." Kathryn explains that this term was used by early Friends to speak about those times when God was working in our lives. For example, meeting for worship would be part of the School of the Spirit. Meeting for business would be another occasion. Kathryn says:

> *There is only one School of the Spirit; it is God (teaching), not us.*

Background

Since she was a child, growing up on Long Island, Kathryn Damiano has always loved silence and solitude. "I had the privilege of having the upstairs of my family home to myself when I was growing up," she says. "A den, a half bath and a bedroom. I learned to enjoy my own company and the companionship of silence." She enjoyed studying there as an adolescent. She remembers talking to herself in Spanish.

"I was religious, but my family was not religious," she says. "My mother did not attend church. My father was Catholic but the Catholic brothers hit his knuckles with their cords to switch him from being left handed, and he never associated with religion again." Kathryn's grandmother took her to the Lutheran church. Kathryn says:

> My parents were surprised that I got religion. . . . When I was thirteen years old I was objecting, in my mind, to the pastors. I was thinking: "God is exciting; you should love God and be in awe of God. This God is boring.

In the 1970s, at the age of twenty, she became a feminist, joined the National Organization for Women, and started a N.O.W. task force on women and religion. At age twenty-six she went to a Methodist seminary in Ohio, and studied feminist theology.

Kathryn has always considered her ministry to be prophetic.

> I went to the seminary when there were few women there, in the seventies. We (women) had our own little population and we got radicalized. It was an empowering situation. We were dealing with institutions that did not want women.

Kathryn has always been one to trust her own authority. Encouraged by a seminary friend who was doing his field placement at the local American Friends Service

Committee office, Kathryn slipped away to attend a Friends meeting. On her first visit, Kathryn remembers sitting next to a "weighty Friend" and noticing that he was quaking. In the meeting for worship, she felt she had "come home." She continued to attend Quaker meeting and became a member of the Religious Society of Friends.

Since that time Kathryn continued her education, with a Ph.D. focused on Quakers of the eighteenth century "Quietist" tradition. She has worked in a number of educational institutions as a therapist, teacher, or staff member. One word she uses to describe herself is "liminal." "Liminal" refers to being on a threshold. Kathryn uses this term to describe her stance both in space and in time. She says:

> This means you live on the threshold, not in the room, not out of the room. You live in the in-between time, in that place of potential. You don't know what is going to happen. You have to live in that place of trust. So you are never in any institution with both feet. In this prophetic stance, you can notice things better than a person who is in the institution. You may say, "Excuse me, there's a dead dog lying in the middle of this room and people are stepping over it; could we look at that?"

She points out that this quality is not always seen as a gift by those in administrative roles. Yet Kathryn continues to ask the questions. She sees the person who is willing to speak the truth, even when no one wants to hear it, as an important part of any community. One of her central questions about a community is: "Are we really the body of Christ?" She says:

> In the body of Christ you need a nose, you need an ear, you need a big toe. If you don't have that understanding, then it is all competitive, which is the world's way.

Soon after she completed seminary Kathryn completed an internship in spiritual direction through the Jesuits. She came to a Quaker center, first as a student, then as a staff member. When she came there, she tried to translate spiritual direction into something Quakers might use. "When I shared this material with the community, I was told that spiritual nurture and spiritual direction were something Catholics do. I was told that it is a priestly role." A group of people joined Kathryn, nevertheless, and began to meet with this focus. Now, fifteen years later, she often hears Quakers saying, "Yes, we do need courses in spiritual nurture." The groundwork laid by the School of the Spirit may have had some influence. Kathryn comments that she often finds herself ahead of the times. "I don't say that in any egotistical way," she says, "because it is not fun. Musicians who are ahead of their time get buried in potter's fields."

The Seed

When there was a shift in personnel at the Quaker center, Kathryn lost her job there. She began to spend more and more time in contemplation. It was at that time that she and Sandra Cronk began to discern the seeds of the School of the Spirit. Other Friends were also interested in bringing this ministry into being. The next question was when to put these ideas into practice. "When do you wait and when do you act?" was the question. "It is easy to fall into waiting too much," says Kathryn. At one point she felt God was saying, "Just get it out there and then I'll work with you." Kathryn comments, "If it comes from prayer, from guidance, it almost doesn't matter when you get out there."

The two women approached their monthly meeting with their idea of offering programs in such areas as spiritual nurture and contemplation. Kathryn wonders how many of the meeting members understood a call to contemplative living and prayer, but the meeting Friends were encouraging. "They told us, 'God bless you . . . go to it,' " says Kathryn. The General Secretary of their Yearly Meeting advised them that what they needed first was a residence." So Kathryn and Sandra began to explore a variety of real estate locations.

It was then that they met with Constance Fitzgerald, a Carmelite Roman Catholic sister, who listened to their story and advised: "You pray. You do not look for places—you pray." She told them to pray for two years. Kathryn states:

> We thought that sounded rightly ordered. It fit who we are and what we felt was our ministry. If we had a place, we would have been getting into changing sheets and providing meals. We wanted to be free of all that. We were clear about the ministry being prayer.

Other teachers joined them. A board was formed, and an organization took shape. It was at that time that Kathryn received a grant from our fund to help support her while she was working towards establishing this ministry. The grant enabled her to drop her second job. This gave her time to work on organizing the new school.

The ministry is under the care of the Worship and Ministry Committee of Philadelphia Yearly Meeting of Friends. A number of programs have been offered over a seven year period, drawing people from all over the United States and from other countries as well. While most of the participants are Friends, there are some non-Friends as well.

How Do You Pay the Rent?

How do you pay the rent while you are following God's leadings? This has been a continuing issue for Kathryn. While Kathryn is administrator and also a teacher for some of the courses of the School of the Spirit, this does not provide her with a living wage. She needs to bring in more money in order to survive economically, to pay rent for her apartment and to put food on the table. A year ago Kathryn had been unemployed for fifteen months, and she was concerned about her finances. She was draining her savings account. She was waiting for God to guide her into the right job. This was very difficult because she had to wait until the right job appeared. When she was offered a job, she had to discern carefully whether it felt right. She listens to her body, to her gut feelings. When a position is not right, she feels it bodily. "It feels like death rather than life," she says. "I've got a stop . . . I'm not going with the living Spirit any more."

For example, Kathryn waited six months for a hermitage ministry position to open up in a Catholic community. There had been an understanding that this position would be offered to her. Yet, when the position was offered, Kathryn felt uncomfortable about the process. There had been very little communication. "I felt I was being asked to do something that was not rightly ordered," she says. As soon as she put down the phone she knew it was wrong. "I felt immediately sick to my stomach, that I was being forced into something. I could feel my immunological system go down. It was as if I would be susceptible to germs that would come along." So she did not take the position.

Although Kathryn believed she had reason to be angry, she noticed she did not feel anger. Again her body gave her clues. "I can do anger," she says, laughing. "I do anger. I've been screaming before about institutions. What came to me (this time) was relief." Kathryn realized she was grateful that God had not put her in another situation where she would live where she worked. When she realized this gift, she was able to let go of the situation without resentment. She was able to sit down and talk with the people without rancor.

After this position fell through, nothing else appeared for months. Sometimes friends would suggest ways Kathryn could go about looking for work. Kathryn had learned by experience that, in her case, those attempts would likely be futile. She has to wait. She said:

> It feels like God will provide the connections and the circumstances; when they show up, then you take them and go with it. It's a different mode than we usually talk about. It is scary.

As the money began to run out, Kathryn would find herself questioning the whole process. She would ask herself: "When I get down to $33.50, then do I go back to the worldly way of doing things?" She observes, "Those are the demons that nip at my heels."

She admitted she was often drawn to despair. "I ask, 'Am I fooling myself? How long can I wait?' " She spoke of "excruciating loneliness." Yet, she said, "If I can stay in that place without filling it in an addictive way, it is transformed into solitude by God. This is God's grace, and I cannot make it happen."

Kathryn calls it "holy despair." She knows that holy despair has always been an essential part of the spiritual path. She points to the journal of George Fox, one of the founders of the Religious Society of Friends.

> George Fox was in holy despair; he was empty. That is when Christ came to him and he knew there was one, Christ Jesus, who could speak to his condition. This is the foundation of our whole (Quaker) spirituality. You are emptied. You are in holy despair, and that is when you are filled with Christ.

Kathryn continued to remind God, "I know you will provide for me . . . you have promised." She said:

> I argue and wrestle with God, and call God to accountability. I even see God as a husband. I say, "God, you have called me not to be married to a human husband, and I trust that you will be the provider.

The good side of this period of unemployment was time for contemplation. "I was moving into a deeper and deeper rhythm. I think I never felt so close to God before. I was sinking deeper into that solitude and it confirmed my calling to a life of prayer and solitude."

While Kathryn was wondering how she would be able to continue to pay the rent, she received an unexpected gift. The Quaker at whose home she rented an apartment came to her with the offer to cut her rent because she believed in what Kathryn was doing. The woman, who is about the age of Kathryn's mother, told Kathryn, "I can feel the prayer coming through the floor boards." Kathryn was very appreciative.

Some income came in from leading retreats, teaching, and providing spiritual direction in individual sessions. A position opened up for her to offer spiritual nurture at a Quaker study center. Although the pay was very low, she was given meals and other compensations. "I was thrilled," she says about this position. It allowed her to do the kind of work she feels called to do. Kathryn says:

> Once you are called to solitude you have to be open to how God will provide that to you. You might have the idea it has to be in a cabin in the woods of New Hampshire. But it may be in my own apartment with a work situation that allows for quiet time and a chance to be with people in a place where there is worship.

Two people who had been through her Contemplative Living and Prayer Program heard that she was working with very little salary. They told her:

> It doesn't sound like you are making much at this job, but we know that you are doing very good work. We have quite enough on which to live, and we would like to pay the rest of your rent.

Kathryn was touched. She accepted this gift, although the part of her that prides itself in being self-sufficient felt tender. She comments:

> I have learned more deeply the contemplative practice of receiving, the vulnerability of receiving. I have to be open to receive from others.

She is also becoming more aware that the practice of receiving stimulates the generosity of other people.

Spiritual Practices

When asked about her spiritual disciplines, Kathryn responds, "From a contemplative point of view the disciplines choose you instead of you choosing the disciplines. Out of the listening, the disciplines become evident." She advises people who are beginning to follow the spiritual path to stick closely to their chosen disciplines. "Later on," she says, "when you get better at listening to the call, the disciplines choose you."

Kathryn says:

> When I spend more time in solitude, journaling takes on a much more important role. That is my only means of expression; it is prayer. I am a very disciplined person otherwise; I am a jogger, a swimmer, and have been a vegetarian for more than twenty years. The physical things, exercise and diet, center me so other things fall into place. Those are fundamental for me.
>
> The main focus for my life is solitude and prayer. I am drawn into prayer when God wants it to happen.

Whether she is doing dishes or making her bed, she is always listening for when God is calling her into prayer. "There is intentional time as well," she says.

So there is both, for intercession and meditation. Your life becomes a ritual, such as brushing your teeth and the pace with which you are doing it. The pace you live your life becomes your discipline. You are not running around like a maniac, because when you are doing that, you aren't listening to God. The discipline is not, "Now I am doing a discipline, and now I am living." One's whole life becomes a discipline.

Intercessory prayer (prayer for other people) is one of Kathryn's regular practices. Kathryn thinks of intercessory prayer as "becoming one with the prayer that is already being prayed for the best for that person." She says:

I know God is praying for that person. God is praying all the time. God is praying, and I join God in God's prayer. So God needs my prayers. I believe God is not omnipotent and that when I join my prayer with God's prayers, I give power to God.

Teaching as a Form of Prayer

She sees teaching as a form of prayer. One of the courses offered by The School of the Spirit, "On Being a Spiritual Nurturer," is structured so people can come from a distance, staying at a retreat center during several weekends over the course of two years. "The main thing we do is pray for these people that are in our responsibility for this short period," she says.

The teaching is more than content. The quality of listening (on the part of participants) has increased over the years we have been teaching. People are listening from a different place. Ministry is evoked from me because of the quality of listening in people. It brings it out of me. I think people recognize the prayer, that we are people who practice a spiritual path. It is not just words or history, we are sharing a place of being. What we are teaching is being. We could almost read from the phone book; what the students are picking up on is the prayer place.

When we have folks in a program for two years, it is like setting a table for people and inviting people to the feast. God's doing the work. It is a different kind of teaching, being who we are called to be authentically. People pick up on that, and then they live authentically. You often see changes in people's lives as they are called to some kind of ministry.

One thing that often happens to participants in the School of the Spirit is they begin to look at words such as "salvation," "atonement," or "resurrection," and find their own authentic understanding for those words. Kathryn says many folks come into the program not using Christian language. By the end of the program this may change. One of the recent participants lost his brother in an accidental death not long ago. When he told Kathryn about the experience of going to the memorial service and sitting in the rain with his brother's wife, the participant said he felt "pressed into the wounds of Christ." Kathryn comments that this participant probably would not have used that image prior to the course. Kathryn exclaims, "When I hear that, I receive."

Participating in the Life of Christ

Kathryn has struggled with her own understandings of Jesus. When she was in seminary and strongly feminist in outlook, Kathryn remembers:

I questioned whether a male savior could save women. What I heard (from scripture) was that the Kingdom of God was within us and among us. I had a teacher in seminary that talked about the community as Messiah. This shifts the understanding of Jesus being Messiah to the community being our salvation. I don't become whole unless you become whole, and we will all become whole, or saved, together.

When I studied eighteenth-century Friends, I saw that this is what they were about. They talked about the community, the Kingdom of God being on earth now. They believed that Christ would be manifest on earth if we live faithfully. It is not only in the sweet bye and bye, but right now.

My way into Jesus is to identify with Him. When my experiences are similar to those of Jesus, I get little glimpses of his life, the loneliness, his being different in a society, his not having a home or children or a "career." I identify with Jesus Christ being rejected, humiliated, falsely accused, failing, knowing the limitations of people and knowing the limitations of human justice. Then I think this life is being replayed in me, not in some external story. It is my story, and Jesus is walking it with me again. It is very real to me; it is not removed. I call it, "participating in the life of Christ."

Does the Leading End or Shift?

The Ministry of Prayer and Learning devoted to the School of the Spirit continues to evolve. One of the teachers moved to Ohio. Another one is moving in the direction of more contemplation and less teaching. At a recent board meeting, the board listened as Sandra and Kathryn reviewed the history of the School of the Spirit, listening for where God was present, where the ministry might have strayed from the leading, and where it has been brought back. The board identified prayer as the main ministry and also committed to join more fully in that ministry of prayer.

Because the teachers have worked so closely with people, they are often called upon for prayer in times of stress. Now that the other teachers are less available, Kathryn says, "I'm the person people call up and say, 'My mother just died. I need you to pray for my mother.'" Kathryn reports that she is feeling "greatly burdened." She says, "It is on my shoulders."

Because she is feeling overwhelmed by these demands, she has been taking this to prayer. She is receiving some answers. "Maybe I am not supposed to allow it to fall on me," she says. "Maybe I am supposed to surrender that. God is saying, 'Okay, that is why I prepared this board, to companion you. It is the board with which you have to share the burden.' " Kathryn does not know how the board will react, but she knows they will be with her in prayer.

"The leading shifts," says Kathryn. "Our first program, 'On being a Spiritual Nurturer,' had twelve people and the last one was fully booked with a waiting list. But inwardly we are not really there anymore. So how long do you continue to do something when that is not where you most are? We can still do it, and people will still benefit from it, but where we are inwardly is much more this place of prayer, to pray for the world and to radiate the love of Christ."

Kathryn says:

> We still do not know what is to become of us, but it was confirmed that our main ministry is prayer. It may move away from doing programs. In church history, when there is a time of church renewal, there are people called particularly to the life of prayer who are praying for the church. Whether Quakers would ever go for anything like that, I don't know. Because Friends are so action oriented, many Friends think spiritual practice necessarily leads to action.

Kathryn asserts, "Spiritual practice makes right all our actions." Kathryn sees prayer itself as an active ministry: "I believe prayer is the most enduring way to change the world."

When asked how her ministry has been supported, Kathryn asserts:

> God has been our support all along. Certainly people give contributions, but the main support is God. We have had challenging times, and we are always thrown back on God. When the ministry is prayer, this is something no one can take away from you. Somebody can close down your program. There are always those demons and threats that throw you back on God. My demons are those things that draw me away from God: insecurity and worries on the inside, such as, "Can I do this?" or "Will I eat cat food in my old age?" as well as threatening situations on the outside.

More and more, she feels drawn to a more contemplative life style. She says:

> When you move more into the contemplative place, you move more away from the personal interaction. Perhaps the whole ministry is moving in this direction. We are called to pray for a monthly meeting, for the Religious Society of Friends, or for the world. I believe the Religious Society of Friends is moving from that interactive focus on experience to the mystery, to the unknowing. I think Sandra and I are preceding that and are drawing other people along into that.

Blessings

It has been very satisfying for Kathryn to reap the fruits of the last seven years.

When I go to residential meetings of Philadelphia Yearly Meeting or Friends General Conference I see people, who have been through the School of the Spirit programs, who are in leadership roles or are doing good things in hidden kinds of ways. People say to me, "I could not have gotten through the death of my mother if I didn't have that experience at the School of the Spirit."

Kathryn comments on her calling to the contemplative life.

The blessing is deeper union with God. The gift of these last several months has been waking up in prayer. And being drawn into prayer when God wants that, living a life style that allows that to happen. The blessings of a lifestyle of prayer is a deeper union with God.

V. SUPPORT FROM FAITH COMMUNITY

Jill Horton-Lyons and Jim Lyons

Jim Lyons and Jill Horton-Lyons

That is not to suggest that we can live harmlessly, or strictly at our own expense; we depend upon other creatures and survive by their deaths. To live, we must break the body and shed the blood of Creation. When we do this knowingly, lovingly, skillfully, reverently, it is a sacrament. When we do it ignorantly, greedily, clumsily, destructively, it is a desecration. In such desecration we condemn ourselves to spiritual and moral loneliness, and others to want.

—The Gift of Good Land, *Wendell Berry*

*I*t is early November on this windy ridge in western Massachusetts. Jim Lyons and Jill Horton-Lyons are putting their cows out to pasture. This couple runs an educational farm as part of a Quaker Conference Center. Jim, a heavy-set man with a quiet, warm manner, wears a red plaid shirt over his jeans as he leads the mother cow, Larissa, out towards a field of high grass. Jill leads the calf, Lydia. I walk along with her while she talks enthusiastically about how the children who come for their farm programs love watching her milk the cow. Jill wears high boots, jeans, and a warm orange vest over her gray sweatshirt on this chilly afternoon. Jill's blond hair is pulled up in a bun behind her head and tucked under a knitted wool cap. While Jim stakes out the cows, Jill points to the sheep being bred in the breeding pen across the way. She tells me that in mid-March these sheep will birth their lambs and that families with children will be coming to stay overnight, having a chance to hold a small lamb, or even give a lamb a bottle. If they are lucky, they may be present for the miracle of birth.

Circling round us are the couple's three dogs, Kate, the old border collie, Bessie, a Jack Russell terrier, and Abby, a large, friendly gray dog. All the dogs are good with children, Jim tells me, adding that this is a requirement for Winterberry Farm. Families with children take part in programs and visit the farm nearly every day.

Back at the farmhouse, we pass the duck pen and the rabbit hutches. Jill takes out a fluffy white angora rabbit and cradles it like a baby. We walk through the porch where Jill is drying cotton yarn which she just finished dying with dye from the bark of the sycamore tree on the hill. Inside the kitchen there are wonderful smells from the soup Jim has been cooking. In the kitchen sink is a large milk bucket ready for tonight's milking. A spinning wheel sits in the corner of the living room, used by Jill to spin wool from the sheep or the angora rabbits. We settle down around the table to talk about what led this couple to be farmers and teachers.

Their story represents how a leading can find its fruition when an entire faith community embraces it. Douglas Steere, in his introduction to Quaker Spirituality *(p. 22), writes about the way early friends cared for one another:*

> *The hospitality they showed to each other knew no bounds, nor did the tenderness with which they treated each other and watched over each other's inward growth.*

Marty Walton speaks of the importance of today's Friends Meeting communities and relationships between the individuals who make up our meetings.

> *What our meetings provide for us is a community that can help us tap into the power of love. Our meetings can call for it and nurture it, first of all in the silence in which we find our center and sit in openness, and then in the guidance for next steps that we've discerned in that living silence. Feeling God's presence working in our lives lets us much more easily look at our fears and choose to let go of them. Feeling the loving support of others puts a human face on "unconditional love" and gives us the strength to work directly with that which we previously had feared.*

The Call

Jim and Jill have not always been farmers. The journey to do this work has been long and circuitous. When the couple first met, at Brown University in the late sixties, Jim was working nights as a security guard to put himself through college. He had just returned from serving in Vietnam and was sufficiently upset by that experience that he helped to start a chapter of Rhode Island's Vietnam Veterans against the War. He continued his interest in Eastern mystical religion by majoring in Chinese intellectual history. Jill was majoring in religion and English. Jill says of her major, "Religious Studies was intellectual. I had no clue about this faith stuff. I was disconnected in many ways."

Although each one had been brought up in mainline churches—Jim's family was Presbyterian and Jill's was Congregational—neither one continued to attend church during college. Jill says:

> As a kid, church was really important to me. I loved the music. I was in Sunday School and Youth Group. My parents were uncomfortable because of its importance to me. You were not supposed to take it seriously.

It was during one high school summer when Jill became an exchange student and lived with a family in Japan that she experienced what she calls "connectedness." She says, "Living in this wonderful family I got to know people who were connected spiritually, intellectually, and in a family living way." For Jill, this became a touchstone experience. She comments, "Later, when I met this connectedness, I recognized it, and had a name for it."

After college, in 1971, the couple married and soon had a child, Megan. Jill took an MBA in health administration, and Jim worked in campus security.

The couple moved to Pennsylvania where Jim became Chief of Campus Police at Swarthmore College. Jill got a good position in health care, managing a group practice for a medical school.

They were both successful in their careers, but something was wrong. It was Jill who became aware of it first. She found herself drinking more than she should. She started attending Alcoholics Anonymous and found it spoke to her condition. Today she is open about stating, "I have been in recovery for eleven years." It was A.A. that opened Jill to God.

Looking back, Jill says:

> This experience is something I have come to under-
> stand as a gift, because it was a breaking through,
> a letting in of pain. It was almost like God saying,
> "Pay attention; pay attention; this is awful. You are
> not living your life. You are not listening. You are not
> being faithful."

Jill realized she needed to make some changes. Alcoholics
Anonymous gave her permission to be herself.

"I always wanted to be a farmer," says Jill. When she
gave herself permission to look inside, she affirmed this
desire as legitimate. Jill's own mother grew up in a farm
family, but she had told her children not to go into farming
because it was a hard, lonely life without much financial
security. Jill says, "In my family, it was important to figure
out something practical to do. Passions were to be taken
with ten grains of salt."

Now that she was facing herself honestly, she recalls,
"I was coming to terms with wanting to be sober and realized you only get one life and boy, you had better . . ." Jill
did not finish the sentence. Instead, she mused, "I wanted to
raise some animals and see how that went."

At that time Jill probably would not have called this a
"leading from God." Was this simply a deep personal desire? Who could know that this seed that had lain dormant
in Jill's heart since childhood would one day grow into a
sturdy tree that would nurture animals, children, parents,
grandparents, and all who came. What would it take for this
seed to germinate, put down roots, and begin to grow?

Farming in Leverett

One of the first lessons Jill learned in A.A. was to ask for
help. "Share," she says. "When you are stuck, admit it and

share." She shared with Jim her deep desire to get out of the city and move to New England. Jill found a job at the University of Massachusetts working in health care management and Jim became Director of Public Safety at Hampshire College. Megan, age twelve, was enrolled in public school. The family purchased a home in the country. The land was wooded and rocky, not good for vegetables, but Jill thought it might be fine for sheep once it was cleared.

This is where Jim began to get into the act. Trees had to be cut down, stumps pulled out. For this job, they purchased a mule off an Amish farm. Jim says:

> The thing that brought me into the fold was the mule, Amos. He was a big old guy, weighed about a thousand pounds and stood fifteen point two hands high.

Together, Jim and Amos cleared the land. Jim also built the fences and did a lot of the heavy work such as digging post holes.

Jim liked working with Jill on this project. For the first time the couple spent a lot of time together. By this time Megan was almost a teenager and had her own friends and life at school. Jill says:

> Jim and I were really looking for ways to do things together. Our standing agreement had been: "You have your career and I have mine." We were trying to achieve a balance through separation. I don't think that works too well. You end up not having so much in common. Farming is how we really started talking to each other.

Jill loved the farming. She added pigs. They named their farm "Winterberry Farm." She says, "The farming slowed me down. It became a meditation. I began to listen to the universe and to God."

Meanwhile changes in the health care profession eroded the personal satisfaction she received in her job at the University. She says, "Health care management was becoming more and more of a shell game. Work got worse and worse for me, in terms of what I was doing."

After a while, Jill quit her job and worked in a yarn store and did a lot of weaving and custom work. As she began to understand the process of cloth, from sheep to textile, she became excited by this process. She offered programs for the children in her community. To pay the bills, Jill took a number of small jobs. One was to do the bookkeeping for Woolman Hill.

Friends Meeting

It was through their daughter that Jim and Jill were drawn to Mt. Toby Meeting of Friends. At the age of twelve, Megan attended a Quaker summer camp in Maine. After this experience, she wanted to go to Friends meeting, but she did not want to go alone. Jim began to go with Megan to Mt. Toby Monthly Meeting.

Jim was not new to Quaker meeting for worship. For him this was a "coming home." Although Jim's parents took him to Presbyterian Church on Sundays, they sent him to Wilmington Friends School for grade school and high school. He comments upon his schooling among Friends:

> For me it was a particularly formative experience. We started every day with silence and we did business in accordance with Quaker principles. My home life was not really happy, so it was important to me to have that very positive experience at school. That early experience provided the fertile field for the continuing spiritual growth.

For a couple of years, Jim and Megan attended Friends meeting and Jill attended A.A. meetings. Then one New Year's Eve there was a party at the Meeting House. Jim told

Jill, "You are safe; there is never any drinking there." Jill enjoyed the group and began to attend Friends meeting with Jim and Megan.

Jim's Evolving Spiritual Journey

Going to meeting every week began to have an influence on Jim. He began to question his career in law enforcement. He had mixed feelings about carrying a gun.

Then Hampshire College, in an effort to save money, began to downsize. Jim's job was eliminated. "This was a watershed time," says Jim. "I had to make a decision as to what to do next." Jim embarked on a national job search and came up with several good opportunities in the security field, including an excellent police chief job in Oregon. Yet he hated to leave the community where he and Jill had put down roots. Jim asked for a clearness committee from his meeting to meet with him, pray with him, and ask him questions to help in his discernment process. Jill was invited to participate in some of the meetings.

One question was, "What aspect of law enforcement do you particularly enjoy?" Jim recalls answering that he liked "helping people and being useful, helping people solve problems, working with them, the soft side of law enforcement." Jim made the decision not to take the police chief job and not to go to Oregon. He says, "I decided I wanted to stay here in Massachusetts with this meeting community and the farm."

Jim found work that satisfied him as a case worker in the mental health field. He has ten or eleven clients who have been diagnosed with severe mental illness, often schizophrenia. He sees them individually each week, often several times a week. When they have crises, he is there for them. For the last six years he has been doing this work through a local agency.

Jill began to work in mental health as well, doing vocational teaching. Now the two of them work for the same agency. Jim works full time and Jill works part time.

Taking a Leap of Faith

Jim was asked to be on the board at a nearby conference center. When the people living in the center's farmhouse decided to leave, Jim and Jill had the chance to move to the farm, bring their animals, and begin to offer programs on spinning, weaving and farming—the same kind of programs they were already doing at their home and in their home community of Leverett. By this time Megan was off at college.

Jim says:

> When we were in Leverett, the farming was Jill's thing, not mine. But when we came up here, we made a commitment together. We were seeing if we could basically stand working with one another. We were really afraid of that.

The couple had a lot of uncertainty. Jill says:

> We were not sure that our call was real. We were not sure if others shared our hunger to know the earth better, or if they would come to programs. We were not sure if the Woolman Hill board or staff understood and supported the programs we wanted to develop. We did not know if we could find energy and strength to farm and to offer programs in addition to our work for pay. We were not sure about our teaching skills. We did not know if we could work together well.

In spite of all their uncertainties, Jim and Jill took the leap of faith. They moved to Woolman Hill. Jill comments:

The first couple of years were really hard. We have big egos; we are both stubborn. We are very respectful of everyone else in the world except each other. It has been hard to learn to be respectful and loving.

Gradually the couple has learned how to work together and learned how to offer the kinds of programs that visitors want. Winterberry Farm now has two dozen sheep, a number of chickens, ducks, rabbits, and a milking cow. The Farm offers day programs, such as "Muffins and Butter," for children and parents, or children and grandparents. They watch the cow being milked, make blueberry muffins, churn cream into butter, and end with a cow story and a feast.

Another one is "Kid's Spin" in which the children spin different fibers such as the fiber from the angora rabbit. During the ten-day lambing season in March, families come and participate in an overnight, hoping to be there for the birth of a lamb. Children help with chores such as collecting eggs from the chicken coop or feeding the ducks or rabbits.

Thanksgiving week is a time when Jim sponsors an open house for twenty or thirty of the mentally-ill people with whom he works, who sit down together over a farm-raised turkey. One June day, Jill and Jim invited a dozen men and women in a pre-release program at the Hampshire County House of Correction to each bring a child to visit.

All these programs grow out of Jim and Jill's understanding of Friends' testimonies of integrity, simplicity, and stewardship of the earth and right use of resources. The farm is just beginning to serve as a place where people can gather to learn, to pray, and to discern about food, about stewardship, about resources and their limitations, and about how we are to live in the coming years. These programs nudge people to ask the questions: Who grew the food we ate yesterday? Where and how was it grown? How did it get here? What prices were paid? How does it matter?

Since the educational program started five years ago, about 4,500 people have visited the farm. Jim and Jill have come to see their work as "ministry." While the programs are extremely satisfying to the couple, the hours of work required have been very demanding. Educational farms such as this do not earn money. To support this ministry, Jim and Jill must work at paid jobs all day, then they come home to do the farm chores. On weekends and special times during the week they offer their programs. In an average week the couple jointly puts in seventy-eight hours of paid work in the mental health field, forty-two hours of farm work, and thirty-two hours of farm program work.

Spiritual Discipline

So how do Jill and Jim manage to keep themselves doing this, day in and day out? I spent the night at Winterberry Farm Bed and Breakfast. When I came downstairs in the morning, I found Jill spinning on her wheel and Jim reading her Psalm 118 from a book that gives them a Bible reading and a commentary each day. Today's reading was, "This is the day the Lord has made. Let us rejoice and be glad in it."

After the reading was finished we all joined the director of the conference center in a fifteen-minute meeting for worship. They do this brief meeting almost every day, even on Sunday before they go to meeting for worship at Mt. Toby Friends Meeting.

Their Friends meeting is extremely important to them. Jill says, "Without our meeting, we would never be here. Meeting has saved us and deepened us. The farming is an extension of our spiritual life. The farm can't get ahead of where we are, spiritually."

The former managers of Woolman Hill, John and Mary Ellen Preston, became mentors for Jill as well as good friends for both of them. Jill says, "From them I learned discipline," says Jill. "I had never understood the importance of spiritual discipline." Jill noticed that they rarely skipped meeting for worship at Mt. Toby. "When one of them had to be at the conference center, the other one went to meeting," says Jill. "We met with them weekly and had spiritual discussions. We talked about living our faith."

> In the beginning we did not go to meeting every Sunday. But after a while the Prestons began to get to me, the whole power of example. If they are doing it, what's wrong with us? I would think, "Maybe we shouldn't worm the sheep this morning. Maybe we should go to meeting and worm the sheep in the afternoon." It was a whole life change for me to set that priority."

The two couples and some other people held a mid-week meeting right at Woolman Hill. Jill says, "We never could have kept going without all this spiritual practice; it is really important."

Mt. Toby Monthly Meeting, as well as the larger community of Friends, has been a tremendous support for Jill and Jim. Particularly supportive has been a small committee at Mt. Toby devoted to this farm ministry. When Jill was asked to serve on overseers of the meeting, she wanted to do this service, but it required a fair amount of time. She says:

> That was really hard because we were doing all this farm work and all this program work. But for me, this was an extension of the discipline. No matter what, the overseers committee had to happen. One of the dangers of following a leading is that we get so pulled into our own little world. As a member of overseers, I realized I had to worry about other people. It was a constant reminder that the world was way bigger than Woolman Hill.

Jim spoke about another important support group, Quaker Farmers. These farmers gather three times a year and share experiences. Jim says:

Farming in our culture is such an odd thing, especially in New England. A lot of farmer's rhythms
conflict with things that are scheduled at meeting.
Most farmers feel estranged.

Recently, Jim and Jill drove to Brattleboro, Vermont, for
a meeting of Quaker Farmers at the home of friends who
have been doing farming for a long time. Jay Bailey is a
mentor for Jim. Jim notes that many of their friends in
Quaker Farmers are also part-time farmers. John Woolman,
a well-known eighteenth-century Quaker, was a part-
time farmer; he had orchards, a trade, and traveled in the
ministry.

Jill comments on the values of this group with whom they
meet: "In some small, or large, way they are living simply
and trying to put themselves in right relationship with God
and with the earth."

Getting Away—Getting Perspective

After five years of working side by side, developing the farm
and the programs, Jim and Jill began to burn out. "We
were stretched nearly to the breaking point," says Jim.
They had proved themselves as farmers and as teachers,
but their lifestyle was back-breaking. They needed to find a
better way. Jill comments:

Developing a leading is so hard. It is hard because it
matters so deeply. Most people don't get to spend
any time working on what is most important. It is the
ultimate gamble, the ultimate leap of faith to put so
much energy into one thing. That is really scary.

Jim points out:

That is really scary to other people too. A lot of what
happens is that we feel so intensely about what we
do that it is hard for people to hear that intensity.

People get embarrassed by it. They react, "Why don't you just calm down . . . take it easy."

The couple wanted a chance to see what other people were doing along these lines. They wanted to travel and visit other Quaker educational farms and conference centers. Yet they did not see how they could leave. They were tied to caring for the animals. They had no money for travel. The conference center, with its own financial struggles, could not help them.

A development day for the conference center was set and a mediator came to work with the Board and staff. The mediator happened to be a board member of our fund, and urged Jim and Jill to apply for a grant to travel among Friends' educational farms and conference centers. Not only did they receive the grant for travel money, they also received a commitment from their Mt. Toby Friends Meeting to take care of the animals while they were gone.

Travel

Jill and Jim took a number of trips. They visited Friends schools, Friends conference centers, and small Friends farms. Jim particularly enjoyed a visit to Westtown School in Pennsylvania where the head of the school, Tom Farquhar, took time for them and showed great interest in what they are doing. Jim was pleased to hear that the Head of this fine Quaker school has a very strong desire to include environmental education in every grade of his school. He has taken steps to ensure in the vision and planning for the future that none of the six hundred acres will ever be put into development.

Jill spoke of visiting Scattergood School in Iowa and meeting Ken and Belle Henshaw. Ken is Head of the school and Belle is the farmer. "We had really good talks with them. We had a shared sense of mission."

Jill says, "It was good to see how they work together in a couple partnership." Belle is in charge of the farm and talked with Jill about struggling with machinery. Jill says, since the trip, "I feel Belle is with me when I look at that tractor and try to figure it out."

The couple traveled to Quaker conference centers, such as Pendle Hill, where they talked with grounds-keepers and a weaving teacher. This travel expanded Jim's and Jill's understanding of educational farming. Having talked to so many people about this work, they see it in a new light.

Jill and Jim are trying to use what they have learned to create a plan for the future. So how do they do it? Are they to expand the farming ministry and lay down some of the work with people who have mental illness? Are they to shift their work so the people with mental illness can participate more in the farm? Jill comments that this mental health work also feels like a response to a "call."

They are seeking ways to strengthen their faith, which is the core of their farming ministry. Yet one of their big questions is how much to talk about their faith and about Friends testimonies with non-Friends who are participating in the programs. Jill mentions a few of these basic values:

> Integrity seems to be an interweaving testimony. Certainly simplicity. Right relationship with the earth and with other people. The other thing is a ministry of hospitality, just welcoming other people in.

The visioning goes on. Winterberry Farm is blossoming. The work is hard; the hours are long; yet the blessings are abundant. As Jill puts it:

> The biggest blessing is the earth and the chores and the animals and the sunrises and the stars and the people. There are so many kids in our life. It is neat in middle age to have all these kids.

VI. MENTORS

Faith Lowell

Faith Lowell

Wild Geese

You do not have to be good.
You do not have to walk on your knees
for a hundred miles through the desert repenting.
You only have to let the soft animal of your body
*   love what it loves.*
Tell me about despair, yours, and I will tell you mine.
Meanwhile the world goes on.
Meanwhile the sun and the clear pebbles of the rain
are moving across the landscape,
over the prairies and the deep trees,
the mountains and rivers.
Meanwhile the wild geese, high in the clean blue air,
are heading home again.
Whoever you are, no matter how lonely,
the world offers itself to your imagination,
calls to you like the wild geese, harsh and exciting—
over and over, announcing your place
in the family of things.
*   — Mary Oliver*

*F*aith Lowell's house in town is easy to find, white with bright purple shutters. At the entrance on a flagpole is a purple flag with a white dove. Inside, two Tibetan Terriers, Dolly and Bianca, greet me with their wavy tails curled up over their backs and wisps of hair over their faces. Faith brings out two small pups, eight weeks old, from the back room. One of the reasons Faith raises this breed is that the dogs are scarce. These were the dogs of the Tibetan Buddhist monasteries before the Chinese took over Tibet. These dogs, thought to carry the souls of the monastery, were considered sacred by the Tibetan people. At the time when China took over Tibet, many of these dogs were murdered along with their monk masters.

Not long after I arrive, the telephone rings. It brings news that Primadonna, one of Faith's dogs who is in a dog show today, has won. Now she, as well as Faith's other two dogs, is an American Kennel Club champion. Faith is elated.

On the refrigerator are photos of Faith's two grown sons, their wives, and children. Faith, divorced, lives alone with her dogs. Now sixty-four, Faith looks and acts much younger. She has an easy way about her, a good sense of humor, a ready laugh. On the walls are poetry, jokes, and pictures. She is dressed casually in sweat pants, a fleece shirt, and Birkenstock sandals. She gives one the feeling that she enjoys life.

Faith has been in private practice of psychotherapy for thirty years. A few years ago, she was nudged into offering group therapy to the women in prison in Burlington, Vermont. Her program, "New Beginnings," is in its fourth year.

Faith has been tremendously influenced by mentors. Following a leading can be a very lonely journey. It takes courage and persistence. To be in touch with a person who has walked that path before can be enormously sustaining. A mentor offers companionship and encouragement for a person nudged by the Spirit.

One of the biggest gifts a mentor can transmit is his or her own spiritual grounding in faith. In On Listening: To God and Each Other *(p. 2), Dorothy Steere says:*

> I recall people I knew as a young girl who were filled with tenderness and love. They had the capacity to listen to me. I sensed a secret knowing, and I began to realize that they were persons to whom Jesus Christ was real and living. They counted on His guidance and they clearly were listening responders to God and to others whom they met. . . . I longed for what they had. They listened and they cared, and I loved them in response.

People who are willing to listen carefully, deeply, and prayerfully are gems. Praying together with one's mentor, in silence and in vocal prayer, can be very important. The worship bonds the three-way relationship—the two people and God— and grounds the action which comes out of the discussions that follow.

In the following story, Faith Lowell speaks about the influence of two mentors. One person she encountered as the leader of a weekend workshop she attended. Even in this short time he had a profound affect upon her life. The other one was a close friend and co-worker as well as member of her Quaker meeting. Although this mentor has died, her words and spirit continue to be a powerful influence for Faith.

Nudged into Prison

Faith is grateful that she was nudged into prison. She says:

> A lot of the blessing is knowing these women. It is interesting that I never forget the name of a prisoner I have worked with. I can forget the name of a client, someone I worked with three years ago or something, but I don't forget these women. I don't know why it

is, but I do know that it is. I really do connect with them. It may be that other people I work with have a chance to set up a support system in addition to me. These women in the prison might have a lawyer who is working for them, but a lot of times, to them, it seems that I am the only one on their side.

Faith carries these women in her heart and thinks of them even when she is on vacation. When Faith traveled to Florida for the Olympics, she sent a postcard back to the women in her prison group. Faith was amazed at how much the women appreciated this small personal gesture. She points out that we never know what is going to be significant for someone else. "This simple act may have been as important as anything I did for these women."

Childhood Memory

Faith can empathize with these women who are in prison. She says:

As a child I felt imprisoned. One of my earliest memories is at the age of four or five, visiting my grandfather's house. There was a dog living next door which was kept in a fenced-in yard. I remember sneaking over and opening the gate and letting the dog out. The whole neighborhood was in an uproar, looking for this dog, but I never let anyone know I did it. Something fenced in has always been a situation I could not stand. I did not understand that until I started doing this work. I was abused as a child. I can identify with being imprisoned and not being in control. People who don't care about you are in charge of your life. Most of the women in prison have also been abused as children. They are continuing this pattern by being in the abusive situation of prison.

Faith comments, "I think everybody has his or her own prison."

Mentors

Faith speaks about two important mentors: Ram Dass and Fay Honey Knopp. She says:

> I think for a large part of my life I really wanted to die. This was my mantra. I would just say to myself a lot, "I want to die." Yes. And now I have a spiritual practice of gratitude.

The pivotal point in this switch came on a seven-day retreat with Ram Dass when Faith was in her forties. "It totally changed my life," she says.

> It was being in the presence of unconditional love for seven days. I had never experienced that before. When I came home from that I did not listen to the radio or watch television or read for six months. I was just in an ecstatic state.

Thinking back on this experience, Faith comments with a laugh, "Instead of having a nervous breakdown, I had a nervous break-up." She explains, " I just felt like I was in a higher state. I knew there was good in the world and that I was loved. It was really an amazing time."

Faith points out that this was different than personal love. "I don't know that Ram Dass even knows who I am," she says, although she has been to several other seven-day retreats with him. Yet she felt his love.

She says, "I didn't have to do anything special or be special in order to be loved. And I knew that I would never lose his love. I don't think there are many people in the world who can give this. For me, Ram Dass is one." This experience had a strong impact on Faith's life. She says,

> It changed my way of living from trying to survive in a hostile world to knowing that I was okay, and that I was going to be okay. I did not know how, but it was okay. I just was going to be okay."

She talks a little more about the healing power of unconditional love. She says:

> As a psychotherapist I basically feel it is my pres-
> ence that heals people; it is not anything that I say. It
> is that I am there. And they know I am there for them.

The other major mentor in Faith's life has been Fay Honey
Knopp. Both women were members of the Middlebury
Friends Meeting. Honey Knopp spent much of her life helping prisoners to make changes in their lives and to find a
more meaningful way to live. She worked with adults who
were molested as children and with sexual offenders. Honey
had friendships with many prisoners around the country.
Honey and Faith became close friends.

Faith was clinical advisor on one of Honey's books. The
two women would talk almost every day. They talked about
whatever came up in their lives and their work. Honey often
talked about working with prisoners.

Honey was in her mid-seventies and Faith was sixty when
Honey took Faith into the Burlington prison. The two Quaker
women met with all the women in the prison. They asked
them what they needed. The women responded that they
needed somebody to help them with their abusive childhoods. Honey and Faith planned a therapeutic program to
be facilitated by Faith.

Faith explains that Honey did not feel qualified to facilitate a therapy group. "Honey staunchly said she was not
a clinician." says Faith. "She never did any therapy with
anyone, except that she did therapy twenty-four hours a
day all her life."

The two women took this proposal to the prison authorities. Faith needed money do this work because it took time
away from her therapy practice. Honey was to write the grant
proposal.

Before she could write it, Honey was diagnosed with cancer and had to go into treatment. She told the doctor she

had to have one week to get ready. In that week, Honey Knopp wrote $100,000 worth of grant proposals for ten different projects, one of which was for Faith to work in the prison. Faith comments, "What kind of person could be diagnosed with cancer and be able to go home and write ten grant proposals in a week before starting her treatment? Pretty amazing!" Honey's death later that year was a tremendous loss for Faith and for all the people Honey touched.

Challenges

Faith had a series of meetings with prison officials to see if the therapy program would be allowed. Faith explains that dealing with prison authorities can be a very challenging part of working with prisoners. She says:

> I could see the prison officials as "them" as opposed to "us." I decided I did not want to do it that way. I did not want to polarize people. I was there to do something helpful for the whole prison environment and that included "them." So that meant to treat them with respect and honor the things they were worried about.
>
> They had legitimate worries. One was that I was going to go and stir up all these feelings once a week, and then the prisoners were going to be "nutso" all week long, and I was not going to be around, and they were going to have to deal with it.
>
> I thought that was a very legitimate concern, so I worked out something in the group. We have a period of time (at the end) when we check out each week. I ask them, "How are you feeling now? If you are feeling upset or angry or whatever, what can you do during the week to carry you through until next week?" That is how the whole idea of giving journals to the women came up. One of the things they can

do is write things down in their journals. Then they have them right there to save until the next week's group session.

Faith continues to keep this attitude of being helpful to everyone in the prison environment. This has meant that the guards have grown to trust her. She says one time she was going in for her group when a guard stopped her and said, "Can I talk to you for a minute? The counselor here has gone home, and there is a woman who is cutting herself. I don't know what to do to help her." Faith talked with the woman, who was not a member of her group, and also to the guard to help him deal with the situation. She says, "I thought it was just a little miracle that he was asking me for help. The impressive thing for me is that the guard trusted me enough to say something to me, even though I wasn't a part of the staff."

Faith says dealing with the prison system is always a challenge:

> Sometimes I go up there and they look at me as if they have never seen me before and make me go through a metal detector. Sometimes I go up there and they give me the key to the room. I never know which it will be. It is not that one of them knows me and the other one doesn't.

Things happen that show how inhuman the system is. Faith used to hold her group between four o'clock and five-thirty. The women would eat dinner then. The group time has been changed and the women now eat at four o'clock. Faith comments, "They do not have another meal until seven the next morning. It is very upsetting to me." Faith does not know why the hour was changed.

Faith doesn't complain to officials. She remarks:

> That is not what I am there for. Besides, if I help the women to just complain, I am not really helping the

women. Life is not fair. So how are they going to live in an unfair world, and unjust world, without getting so angry that they commit crimes?

Faith supports the women taking appropriate steps, such as writing letters to people who are in a position to improve conditions at the prison.

Sometimes the women ask Faith about her Quaker faith. They know that the Quaker meeting has been a major support for this work. What interests the women most is the concept of non-violence. They want to learn how to communicate without making power plays.

Although Honey died three years ago, sometimes Faith feels Honey's presence. Faith says:

> Sometimes on the way home from the prison I talk to Honey. I ask her advice, and she always gives it quite freely. One time in particular I remember one of the women in my group had done something and she was going to be in solitary. I decided that I wanted to see if I could get her out of solitary to attend the group. I had to write a letter to the superintendent. I had a conference with Honey to ask how to write this letter. What she said was, "Don't be emotional. Be very practical."

Faith asserts that Honey was extremely practical and that is one reason why she was treated with such respect by prison officials. Faith just wrote to the superintendent and told him the reason the woman was in solitary was she had drunk some alcohol. Her drinking problem was part of what she was being treated for in my group. It made sense for her to come to treatment rather than just being punished for it. That way she could get some help with that issue. Faith explained to him that this was a particularly good time for the woman to get help.

Faith was amazed at the response. The superintendent called her at home and said he had left orders that the woman could come to the group. He told Faith he realized that at the last minute things sometimes don't happen the way they are supposed to. So he gave Faith his beeper number in case there was some kind of a foul up at the last minute.

Faith commented: "Honey really helped me write that letter."

One Session

At the end of every ten-week session, Faith holds a graduation party for the group, complete with diplomas. Faith asks the women to list their favorite foods, and then she makes the brownies, cakes, and mostly chocolate desserts requested for their party. During her last group, there had been a bottle of vodka smuggled into the prison during the previous week, so a restriction was ordered by the administration: no food at the party.

Faith talks slowly, deliberately, choosing her words:

> I had to work out with the women how could we celebrate without food. What they wanted was to watch a video. They wanted it to be a funny video, a comedy, and they wanted me to choose it. So I went home and thought, "Oh what should I bring?" I did not know what I should bring, but I kept wanting to bring "Ground Hog Day," a movie with Bill Murray. What I did was I took three videos out of the video store as possibilities, and I drove up to the prison. I just decided that the right video of the three would show itself to me. It was, in fact, "Ground Hog Day."
>
> I took it in. I had seen it a long time ago. I did not know why I wanted to show this until I started showing it. The story of "Ground Hog Day" is that a very nasty man is caught in living the same day over and over and over again. He is trapped in the day and the day is ground hog day. And every morning the alarm

goes off at 6:30 and the radio goes on with Sonny and Cher singing "You got me Babe."

Faith laughs as she remembers the video.

> This man, who is a newscaster, is trying to start a relationship with this woman . . . but he is just nasty. And finally he starts to make some changes in the way he is living, in the day. The video goes through the day and shows they go out to a bar, and she will say, "I always toast to peace." So the next day, when they start the day all over again, they go to the bar and he says to her, "I always toast to world peace." And she thinks he is wonderful. He starts to change. So, interestingly enough, the name of my group is "New Beginnings."

After the video was over, the women said, "That's just like us." Faith asked the women, "What do you mean?" The women told her, "We keep doing the same thing over and over, and it never gets us anywhere."

Faith offered a silent prayer, "Thank you, God, you had me choose the right video." Then the women started talking about the fact that if you can't change the world outside you, you have to change yourself inside.

Faith comments:

> It was just like a little miracle . . . out of choosing this video. And I didn't know why I chose it. I feel as if the work I have been doing with these women is guided . . . and I am not in charge of it all the time, but it is okay.

Support

When Faith decided she wanted to run a therapy group in prison, she realized that the time taken away from her private practice would make a big dent in her income. She was not sure she would be able to cover her living expenses. She applied to our fund for help the first two years.

In addition, Faith's Friends meeting minuted support for Faith's prison ministry.

> The meeting is my big support in doing this work. If there is anything that comes up that I am having a problem with, I just gather up a little clearness committee, or I call up two or three people from meeting who are working in prison one way or another, and I run things by them. It is a huge support knowing that the meeting values what I am doing.

Not long ago the meeting had a garage sale and made $700 for Faith's prison ministry.

Spiritual Practices

Faith tells about her spiritual practice of gratitude. She walks over to the fireplace and shows me a carved figure of a Buddha. Faith tells me:

> This is the Buddha of gratitude. In the morning I go stand in front of that little statue and feel glad to be alive. Then I take one of my dogs out for a walk. And I sing. I sing the song "Morning has Broken." And then I have an "Halleluia" song I sing. I make up the words to it as I go along. For example, "The dawn has broken, Halleluia. The whole world awoken, Halleluia." I make up the lines as I walk and they change with the day depending upon if it is raining or sunny or whatever. That is my morning practice. That is how I start the day.

Another spiritual practice is to work with other people on a solstice play, *Night Fire,* about going through the dark to get to the light. Faith is stage manager for this play each year. The story line is different from year to year, for example it might be the Holocaust or the environment, but the basic theme of going through darkness to light is always there. The play is given in a number of communities throughout Vermont.

A friend of the woman who writes and directs the plays went to Bosnia a year ago and took scarves and jewelry to a group of women who had been in rape camps. Those Bosnian women sent back chocolate truffles wrapped individually. These were given to Faith to take to the women in her prison group. The women in prison were very moved by this gift. They refused to eat, or even unwrap, the chocolates. Instead they took the chocolate truffles to their cells and kept them on their shelves.

Prayer is another spiritual practice. Faith says:

> I certainly pray on the way up to the prison. I pray to keep my heart open. There is so much pain in there that I pray not to protect myself from that pain, because these women need somebody to hear it. So many of them feel so hopeless.

Faith has learned over thirty years of therapy how to listen to pain without taking on the feelings. She says, "Every once in a while something sneaks up on me. But usually I am pretty good about that." She comments that these women do not have anyone else to hear them. Sometimes they have case workers, hired by the prison system, assigned to them, but the women often mistrust anyone connected to the system.

Another spiritual practice for Faith is reading poetry. Her favorite poet is Mary Oliver, who wrote the poem at the beginning of this chapter.

How Long Will You Be Doing This Work?

Faith has no idea how much longer she will be doing this work. She says, "I don't know. It feels a little bit like it is quieting down. I don't know if it needs to rest a little."

Faith says that in Vermont there is going to be a change for women in prison. At this time all women are imprisoned in the Burlington prison, which is primarily set up for men. There is little programming for women at the prison in Burlington. Faith says, "All the women do is sit there and be bored."

Changes are coming. Faith reports with satisfaction:

> The women are finally going to have their own prison, in Waterbury. So the women are going to be moved, hopefully in March, to Waterbury, and hopefully they will get some of the services they need.

Recently Faith was one of two people not related to the prison system who were invited to testify for the Governor's commission on Women. The Department of Corrections has decided to establish two halfway houses in Vermont for women coming out of prison, during which time they will have what they call "wrap-around" mental health services. Faith is hoping there will be some vocational training so that the women can leave with some kind of a skill. She made the suggestion that the women be given training in practical skills such as computer work, hair dressing, and landscape care.

Faith does not know whether she will continue her group therapy at the new prison. She says:

> My work might not be needed so much. Or the need might change. If my work in my prison is needed, I will continue to do it. I do not want to do something that is not needed. I don't feel like I have to keep doing it, and I don't feel like I have to end it. I'm just open to following whatever needs to be done.

Faith comments on the nudge to do this work.

> There have been times as this thing has developed that I have said, "Not me, Lord, I don't want to do it; that one, she looks like a good one, she could do it."

Faith has learned much from this leading:

> Just learning to trust what is inside you is a real challenge. You don't always know why you are doing what you are doing. You just know that you are supposed to do it.

VII. FIRST SMALL STEPS

Tom Goodridge

Tom Goodridge and Class

The Milkweed

Anonymous as cherubs
over the crib of God
White seeds are floating
out of my burst pod.
What power had I
before I learned to yield?
Shatter me great wind
I shall possess the field.

Robert Lowell

*T*om Goodridge greets me at the door of his apartment building in Harlem. From the ninth floor he has a clear view between buildings out to the Hudson River and beyond. There is a quality of playfulness in Tom which is expressed in his apartment. On his window sill are some of his special toys, a small rocking horse, a fuzzy lion, a wooden duck, a tiny Christmas tree, and a few stones and shells. On the table are children's books, Goodnight Moon, and others. On the wall he has posted poetry. Tom has invited me to stay in his apartment overnight before visiting his school. He prepares a dinner of pea soup, salad, and sautéed potatoes and mushrooms. After dessert of chocolate-covered halvah, we settle in the living room to talk.

Tom speaks about making the decision to train to teach mentally-retarded children in the challenging setting of a public school in Harlem. Many of us hesitate before we take the first step in responding to God's nudge. We may wonder why we are doing it. "Is the step really God's will or is it something I dreamed up myself?" We may wonder whether we have the ability to carry out this task. We may wonder where it will lead us if we take this first step.

Thomas Kelly, in Testament of Devotion *(p. 60), advises:*

> Begin where you are Use that little obedience you are capable of, even if it be like a grain of mustard seed. Begin where you are. Live this present moment, this present hour as you now sit in your eats, in ut-ter, utter submission and openness toward Him. Lis-ten outwardly to these words, but within;, behind the scenes, in the deeper levels of your lives where you are alone with God the Loving Eternal One, keep us a silent prayer. "Open thou my life, guide my thoughts where I dare not let them go. But thou darest. They will be done." Walk on the streets and chat with your friends. But every moment behind

the scenes be in prayer, offering yourselves in con-
tinuous obedience.

Tom's story illustrates the process of taking the first step,
often in uncertainty, and doing the best job one can, day by
day with God's help. At forty-six, Tom is several years into
his work of teaching mentally-retarded children. Prior to
teaching school, he worked with handicapped adults, setting up group homes for them.

"My work has always been with the folks who fall between the cracks," says Tom.

> I felt these were the children to whom I had the most
> to offer. I don't feel my calling is towards academics.
> I feel it is to liberate the sometimes hidden gifts in a
> child and to create a community in the classroom.
> Working with wild children is an adventure in hu-
> man creativity. Since they are not crusted over by
> our culture's version of civilization, I can touch a
> rawer, nascent humanity open to something outside
> the norm. The ;norm feels mostly like a cage to me.
> Being with thee children forces me to expand my
> sense of what is human and what we are here for.

A Visit to School

Tom packs up marshmallow bunnies for the Easter party at
school. He leads me through the streets of Harlem to his
public school where he teaches a special education class
for the younger children. We pass through a park with a
huge black rock outcropping. Tom shows me that the rock
looks like a whale; he points out the eye is weeping tears
after last night's rain. The whale has been an important
symbol for Tom. When he first discovered this whale, it
confirmed in him that he was in the right place, doing the
right thing.

We duck through a hole in the iron fence and cross a street with heavy traffic. Tom points out that many of his small children must cross this street on the way to school each day. Half way down the block a three-story blue building, the public school, looms on the right. Across the street from the school, tucked in a "vacant" lot between two high apartment buildings, is a garden. Purple crocuses and yellow pansies brighten the gateway. On the gate is a sign, "Garden of Love."

With the pride of a father showing me his first-born baby, Tom leads me into the garden and down a curvy red-brick path between the plants. We pass a pine tree, a red-bud tree, an apple tree, a rhododendron bush, some pussy willows, and wildflowers. At the end of the garden we come upon a circle of logs where we sit down for a few moments before we enter the school. Tom was one of the people who initiated and now cares for this garden. He is grieving the fact that this beautiful garden may be destroyed to make room for development. The city bureaucrats have decided to raise money by selling off a number of such gardens created in city-owned lots. Although many people are protesting, the Garden of Love is currently listed to be sold.

We move into the school where Tom greets his children in the school cafeteria where they are eating breakfast. Breakfast and lunch are served year round, even in summer when the school is not in session. Most of the children and teachers in this Harlem school are black, and I find myself conscious of my own and Tom's light skin.

Tom had told me he was drawn to the African-American child. He had explained, "They have such life in them." Tom had gotten to know a couple from Soweto during a year he spent at Pendle Hill, a Quaker center near Philadelphia. Tom made a trip to South Africa, thinking he might teach there. However, when he visited there, he found no opening. He was overwhelmed by the politics and felt he would be more effective closer to home.

Tom introduces me to the aide and to his seven "mentally retarded" children ages five through nine. Tom gently gathers these children and leads them upstairs to their classroom.

On the wall outside the room is a poster: "Save our Garden." In large capital letters, one of Tom's children has written: "If you put a house in our garden, you can kill the animals, worms, snake, and cat."

Other comments: "I want purple flowers." "I want butterflies." One child has written, simply: "No house there."

Over in the corner is a huge box labeled, "Worms." Isaac lifts the cover and shows me the tiny red worms. He lets a tiny worm walk over his finger, then puts it back carefully into the box. Tom explains, "The worms eat damp shredded newspaper and vegetable peelings. Then they poop out beautiful soil for the Garden of Love."

We sit in a circle. These children are not ready for reading, writing, and arithmetic. The basic curriculum in Tom's classroom is love. The day will include show and tell, singing, dancing, drumming, painting, and listening to stories. It is obvious that Tom has built a lot of trust with these children. This classroom feels like an oasis of safety for these children.

Tom introduces me and tells the children I come from the seashore of New Hampshire. He had suggested that I bring sand and shells with me to show the children. We clap and sing, "Down by the Bay." I show the children the sand, shells, smooth stones, a seagull feather, green sea glass, smelly kelp, and a piece of driftwood.

Saul picks up the driftwood and cries, "A bone—a tree bone." Tom delights in this kind of poetic thinking that his children often do. We set up a foam tray for each child at the play table and let them create their own small scene of the seashore which they may take home.

At one point I notice the odor of bowel movement in the air. Over behind the bookcases Tom is quietly changing a diaper. I'm surprised that none of the other children giggle.

They do not even seem to notice this is going on. In a few minutes the child has been cleaned up and joins the other children at the play table.

Today is the last day of school before Easter weekend. Tom gets out a bunch of hats: fireman's hat, baseball cap, etc. He leads a parade of children hopping along the floor with his hands up like little paws, singing, "Here comes Peter Cottontail, hopping down the bunny trail, hippity hoppity, Easter's on its way." The children follow him, some joining the singing. One plays drums. The parade ends at the snack table. The children are delighted when Tom brings out the surprise—yellow marshmallow bunnies with which to top the usual snack of graham crackers with peanut butter.

The Roots of the Plant

What draws a person towards teaching children such as these, children who, from their earliest years, are marginalized by society ? Tom has always been attracted to the people on the edges of society; first it was handicapped adults and now mentally retarded children. Many people view Tom's work as noble. Tom insists that his work has a shadow side that is not so noble. He points out that in each of our lives there is a part that is visible, a part that is like a plant, growing into the light, flowering and bearing fruit, and then there is the part of the plant that is unseen, that dwells in the mud, the undergirding roots that feed the plant from within. He says:

> The more we attempt to live our ideals, to stare into the light, the greater the shadow we cast. In order to truly honor our leadings we must also confront our dark psychic womb which helped to bear these leadings.

Tom is open about sharing his dark psychic womb. It holds aspects of his psyche that are not so admirable. He says one is fear of intimacy and trust. He has no life partner. Another is a strong sense of superiority as he tells himself, "Hey, I am called by God." Still another is immaturity. He says, "I want to be with children because I don't want to grow up." Lastly he sees that he avoids confronting the powers which most oppress him personally. He comments, "I attempt to liberate oppressed children—surely one of the noblest and safest of callings."

When Tom considers the roots of all this in his own psychic womb, he goes back to his childhood when he was seven, eight, or nine.

> We were up at our summer house in Connecticut where I had a lot of time alone and a lot of time in the woods. I was walking up the log steps to the house when in happened. I can't say I heard a voice, but all of a sudden the words, "You are homosexual" came to me. I did not know what the word meant, but I knew it was bad and it was something to do with sex. It felt like a condemnation. I remember it as very powerful.
>
> It was just too scary to even look at, so I shut down something in me. I closed down. Unconsciously I must have thought that if I was going to develop sexually, go towards that kind of sexual maturity, that would lead to something wrong.

And so Tom has never had a life partner. He has lived alone and given himself to his work. He says:

> I did let people know I was gay, but I was not doing anything about it. I chose to deny my sexuality. Because I judged myself as bad or wrong, I was going to be good.

Tom comments that he has read biographies of other gay men who in their childhoods felt they were bad and decided to be the best little boy to make up for it.

He knows people who have chosen to champion gay liberation, but this is not Tom's way. Instead, he has championed mentally retarded liberation. When he was about seventeen he worked in an institution for mentally retarded people.

> It was a huge state institution full of mentally retarded and other kinds of aberrant people kept in clearly subhuman conditions. It was the most monstrous thing I had ever seen.

While Tom did not blow the whistle on this institution at that time, he spent many years working to liberate people such as that. He went to a place called Camp Hill in Scotland where he experienced the opposite environment, a wonderful community where mentally retarded adults could live free of society's judgments. From there he returned to the United States and set up group homes for the most marginal and "unacceptable" people. He helped to bring them into community and to claim their own lives. He taught them to learn how to travel independently, to get work if they could, to express themselves through the arts. He taught them to make dinner and to do their laundry. He says:

> I chose a liberation that was safe for me. I could be incredibly self-righteous about the right of a mentally retarded individual to have a good life. I was not as clearly able to say, as a gay man, I could have my love and declare it and be honored for that in the world. By my actions I accepted the homophobia of society.

Tom is very likable and has many friends. He says, "Using the same energy some people might have used to find, and bond with, a partner, I have been able to reach out and make connections with far flung humanity." He has been able to relate well to all kinds of people, including those who often do not form relationships easily.

Major Life Change

Tom spent three years starting a group home for mentally retarded adults. Then he took a year off at Pendle Hill to focus on his spiritual journey. He says, "I felt a confirmation that my groping along, listening closely to my heart, would lead me home." When his parents grew ill, he moved and found work near their home in Connecticut. There he continued his work with agencies serving adults with disabilities.

For the next ten years Tom lived with his parents who were both beset with emphysema. Tom says,

> I began to feel very close to death, to have an intimacy with it. I largely lost my sense of myself in the world.

It was Tom's father's death in 1990 that seemed to release Tom to move on. His mother encouraged him, he says. "My mother did keep saying to me, 'Get on with your life, Tom.' I felt I needed her permission."

Not long after that, our country became involved in the Persian Gulf war. Tom felt the war was wrong. He recalls:

> I couldn't believe how everyone around me "knew" this (war) was the right thing to do. I felt very isolated. I fasted. I went to all the Washington peace marches. I had to make a statement that this was wrong.

Nudged by the Spirit

At the age of forty, after his mother's death, Tom went into a major life change. He described it: "It feels like I'm starting again as I reach my middle years. It began with a yearning to live and a belief in my dreams." A number of experiences came together to influence him to make a change in his life.

The first was a workshop, "Council of All Beings," dealing with grieving for the destruction of our environment. He comments:

> This workshop was a relief. I was able to grieve in community. Because of the importance of nature to my spirituality, the loss of the natural world is equivalent to my own death and the death of Earth Mother. With the desperateness of the war and the association with the death of my own parents, I got into this alternative state which was carving out the space for something new.

The second experience was a comment from a friend. " I can remember feeling just very stuck," says Tom. "A friend told me, 'You've got to do something, Tom'." Tom was considering teaching in public school, yet hesitated. Tom realizes he is unconventional in his ideas and he comes from a rebellious family. The thought of teaching in a public school seemed "somehow absurd."

> It was to be in the belly of the beast, the beast that I always sensed even from the outside would be arbitrary, obtuse, and something very wrong.

He was both drawn to the idea and doubtful at the same time. Tom comments on how important it was to him to have some encouragement from his friend at that point. Tom comments, "When my friend said 'You've got to do something,' I needed to hear that."

The third push came during a men's retreat. The participants were asked to prepare for the retreat by conjuring up their own "inner child." Tom says, "I made an image of 'Little Tom' who was about four years old." Later on, when he drove to Bank Street to begin graduate school in special education, Tom remembers telling this little boy, "Tommy, we're gonna put sugar on the table." Tom comments, "It was a way of honoring the little boy in me. I told him, 'We're gonna do it, Tommy.' It gave me a sense that I wasn't just doing it for myself. I could feel that little boy and wanted to do right by him." Tom did not do much testing of this leading.

> I felt pretty desperate. It didn't feel like a matter of choice. It was life or death. You'd better get out and do something. This did not seem like one of many things; (the message) seemed to be, "Get out of that hole. Go there!" It certainly wasn't like the thing where you list the options and advantages of each. It was just, "Somehow there's something there for you . . . do it."

Doubts

Tom wondered about his ability to follow through on his leading. He was not doubtful about his ability to get a master's degree in education. "There was no doubt in my mind that I would love Bank Street (teacher training college) and the discussions on education," he says. "I love talking about education. But the total question was, 'Can I do it (teaching in the city school system)?'" Even after he began his training, doubts plagued him. "My doubts were very well founded," he says. "I'd say to myself many, many, many times, 'What am I doing there?'"

From the reality of Tom's Harlem classroom, Bank Street College seems very far away. Yet it has provided a stable grounding for him as he tested himself in public school teaching. He says:

> Facing that insanity, (Bank Street College) still gave me one foot in a place that was telling me I wasn't crazy. At least one foot was arguing with the other foot.

First Year Teaching

"My first year was wild," recalls Tom. "O my God! And I was deathly afraid of letting anybody know how wild it was." Tom has vivid memories of certain moments. He had one child, David, who was particularly wild. Tom describes one of those times:

> David is running about, going through closets, taking things out, watching how they drop, and so finally I get him and hold him down. Meanwhile my attempt is to continue to do something positive. So while one hand is holding David down, the other hand has a book and I am telling a story to the rest of the children. While David is trying to kick me and kick away the book, one of the little boys drops his pants and has his penis in his hands and is saying, "I've gotta go, I've gotta go!"

Tom told him, "I can't take you now." Tom recalls, "I was imagining my principal coming in at that point unannounced."

One of the most difficult children to handle was Danny. Tom had him during his first three years teaching. When this child finally moved on to the next class, the more experienced teacher referred him promptly to a school for emotionally disturbed children. Tom says:

> I did not refer him because I felt I should take whoever came to me. Somehow they were meant to be mine. If I couldn't do it I was a failure. I couldn't call out for help or else they would realize I was an incompetent teacher and get rid of me. The system encourages a sense of isolation because that is what allows a teacher to do what no one should have to do.

Now five years into the job, Tom has gained experience and knows how to handle situations better. He recognizes which children ought to be in the emotionally disturbed classes rather than in his classroom.

Survival

Tom finds solace in journal keeping. During his first year teaching, he says, "I would come home each day and write. I was dazed. I kept a record of my chaotic days, not knowing yet how to respond to the chaos in my students' lives."

Tom remembers this story vividly:

> One day David told me he had found a dead cat and brought it into his house and put it into his bed with him. He'd never had a pet, and it was something important to him. I tried to honor the spiritual experience he had with the once-living animal and to separate that from my fear of disease and other things that come with it. This kind of experience was more difficult than anything I had ever imagined. Yet the life and spirit in these children totally drew me to them in spite of all these horrors.

Tom recalls that he was exhausted, but that he dug down into resources he did not know he possessed. He was not only teaching school but also going to graduate school. On weekends he was going home to be with his mother who was very ill.

One practice that was helpful to him was in the morning he would lie in bed and visualize the Light going into every part of his body. He talks with God a lot. He says, "I have morning dialogues with God. Mostly they are monologues. I do have a strong faith." Tom believed from the start that he was attempting to do what he was meant to do. "This belief was sustained," he comments.

Another practice that he loves is doing "the salute to the sun," a yoga series of movements. Going to the park to be with the trees is refreshing and sustaining for him. Tom likes the city, in spite of the fact that he misses walking in the woods and swimming in the lake, as he could do at his parents' suburban home. He says, "Here in the city I feel this strange energy of life and diversity."

Community

Tom relies on his spiritual community for support. "Morningside Friends Meeting is my community," says Tom.

> I knew I needed that. I came to them and said, "I'm here to be a part of this meeting." I'd never done that before at any meeting, but I was feeling, "I'm going to let down some roots into this place."

A former public school teacher happened to sit next to Tom at his first meeting for worship at Morningside Meeting. Tom told her he was planning to teach in this school. She responded, "They don't want you. They want blacks." This woman had been a teacher for thirty-five years and got pushed down the stairs at her last assignment. She had had some horrific experiences.

Tom says, "It discouraged me a little, but I was dumb enough to not listen to her." The two of them became friends and she loves to listen to Tom's stories from the classroom.

"I define myself, first, in spiritual terms," says Tom, "so I regularly try to make meeting for worship. It is important to me." He is also co-leader of the Friends in Unity with Nature committee at his meeting. Although he usually avoids committee work, Tom couldn't resist the link between the ecological and the spiritual.

Meeting for Worship in the Garden of Love

Tom's Meeting Friends understand how he feels about the possibility of losing the Garden of Love. Tom says, "They feel

125

my discouragement now and it's scary to them." The Friends joined Tom in the Garden of Love for meeting for worship. They sat on the stumps and shared, out of the worship, what nature meant to each of them. Tom relates, "Some of the children came in at that time and must have thought we were a little peculiar, sitting there quietly on the tree stumps."

Tom says:

> I'm thinking if they do cut down those trees and build on that lot I will have to ask myself if it is time to leave. That is the only part of the school I really could believe in.

He speaks of "that box of a school" and how separated it is from the community.

> It is part of the wrong that education has evolved into. But our direct encounter with nature . . . that is real. It's trees. It's a little bit of wild nature."

Tom says that the origin of the idea for the Garden of Love was partially provoked by one of his young students. Tom took his group to Morningside Park, "a pretty grubby park on the margin of Harlem." Jimmy looked up and said, "Look at all the trees together."

This comment showed Tom that Jimmy had never been to the woods, had only seen trees marching in military order at the edge of the streets. What a contrast this was from Tom's own childhood when he was able to climb trees and run amuck. Trees gave him great solace as a child.

"These children are up against it," says Tom. "They have no where to run to. At home there is MTV pumping out its stuff." The Garden of Love means a great deal to these children, reports Tom. "The trees are taller than us now."

Does This Leading Have an Ending Time?

Tom is feeling discouraged by the threat to the Garden of Love. He does not have a clear leading about how long to stay teaching here. "I know I need children in my life," says Tom.

> I love the children best who fall through the cracks. I do feel a particular kinship with them, and with an education that is built on play and natural curiosity. But I may jump this ship.

There are both blessings and challenges for Tom in this job. He speaks of wonderful moments such as singing "Here comes Peter Cottontail hopping down the bunny trail" and leading the parade, hopping through the classroom. "Whenever I am able just to move, I start dancing in class," he says.

Tom's great fear, going into this job, was that he wouldn't be able to handle the children. He had many doubts. "Can I make it in this world? Can I do it?" He says:

> If I couldn't make it with the Board of Education of the New York City school system I could still feel I was redeemable, but if I couldn't make it with these little wild, free kids, then I would doubt myself. If I didn't think I had this touch with children, then that would totally obliterate my self-esteem. I felt it was deeply part of who I am that I should be with these children. Maybe that's why I clutch to this work so desperately.

When asked to answer the question, "Have you made it in this world?" Tom responds:

> It depends upon when you ask me. There are times when I accept other people's definitions and think, "You are not doing what you are supposed to be doing. You are a poor excuse for a teacher." Other times it might be the other way. I say to myself, with a lofty feeling, "You know what you are doing with these kids; don't worry about what others think."

One of Tom's queries is whether or not he should be part of a school system that seems so alien to his own values.

He says:

> The public school system is not a place to liberate
> souls. It is almost the opposite of that. A deep part of
> me asks, "Should I be a part of this?" When I look at
> it from a later perspective, am I going to be proud
> that I was a part of that?

He states, "When you know something is wrong, you
should go and build something that's right."

So Tom is struggling with the question, "Will I know when
the test is over? When I am supposed to go on?" He longs to
be a part of a community. He would like colleagues who
understand him. He says,

> I do largely dismiss the judgment of my supervisors.
> The things they are judging me on are not things I
> have any stake in or concern for. Sometimes I feel
> like a gyroscope. I can go right out of whack be-
> cause I have no alignment with the school. I would
> like to be in a place where I am somewhat under-
> stood for what I am doing while hopping down the
> bunny trail.

As he looks back on his experience of following his
leading to teach in the city's public school system, Tom comments, "Despite all the insults of the system, there are
times when I am with one of my children and we look into
each other's eyes. I feel I am confirming and I am being
confirmed."

Situations change. A new principal is coming into the
school. A new therapeutic model has been adopted, closer
to Tom's approach in his classroom. Tom hopes that he may
feel less isolated.

Gradually Tom is beginning to make a shift in his own self
image. He says, "I no longer want to live out of denial." He is
trying to honor the parts of himself that he has repudiated.
Tom is in a process of integrating parts of himself, accept-

ing the broken parts, the shadows, and the competing voices, many of which he has often denied. As Tom moves into a deeper wholeness, this inner wholeness will no doubt find expression in his outer life and work.

Postcript

Not long after this interview bulldozers came one dark day without any warning and destroyed "The Garden of Love," making way for an apartment building to be erected. It was legal. The land belonged to the city of New York. If the city wanted to sell it, it could. But it happened so fast that Tom and the others had no chance to transplant the trees and flowers.

It was a sad day. I wondered if Tom would quit the job. But he didn't. He is still there with those children. Not long ago Tom telephoned me to say, "We are going to plant another garden." This time it is on school ground. The Garden of Love refuses to die.

VIII. PILGRIMAGE

Martha Penzer

Stella, Martha, and Victor Penzer

Mother's Day

A gray slab,
an after-thought,
rests on that morning
of august 19, 1942.
    the bullets that killed you
    made my survival
    a crime.
I reach into the mass grave:
Mama, tell me
I am a good girl.

by Stella Slawin Penzer

*I*t was a warm February day when I drove to Boston to interview Martha Penzer at the home of her parents. Martha, age forty-five, was on a ten-day vacation from her job as a high school teacher in Slovenia. Her parents live in a suburb of Boston. I was planning on interviewing Martha on her experience of participating in the Pilgrimage for Peace and Life.

How appropriate it was to meet Martha at her parents' home in Newton, Massachusetts. It was her parents' personal history as Polish Jews during World War II which propelled Martha to go on a "Pilgrimage for Peace and Life." Martha's mother, Stella, had been a nursing student in Poland when the war began. Her whole nursing school had been forced to move into the Warsaw Ghetto. Stella showed me, with great tenderness, a nursing pin her teacher saved for her and gave her after the war. Stella talked freely about those terrible days in 1942 when her whole community in the Otwock Ghetto was rounded up and murdered. Stella escaped when a friend gave her false identification papers. She fled to the southern Poland city of Lwow where there were some Armenians who had darker skin and hair, where she hoped to hide. Even there she was at risk, so she moved on into Eastern Czechoslovakia. Stella lived under false papers until the end of the war.

Stella's twin brother also was given papers but he was not so fortunate; he was recognized as a Jew and gunned down by a Polish policeman. Stella walked with me around the living room, showing me photos of her family members who were killed during World War II.

Martha's father, Victor, had spent the war years in Auschwitz-Birkenau death camp and was one of the few who survived until liberation. In the last few days he was force-marched with other prisoners to Mauthausen Prison Camp from which he was liberated. Stella and Victor met and married in Munich after the war then moved to a Boston suburb where Victor practiced dentistry in an office *connected to their home until he retired ten years ago. For Victor and Stella, memories of the holocaust remain vivid and haunting. Their response to these memories has been to work for peace and reconciliation. Martha and her sister and brother were raised in this home, absorbing, as children do, the memories and thoughts of their parents.*

Martha wore a brown print cotton dress, knee socks, and clogs. Her thick, black curly hair was pulled into pigtails. Around her neck was a multicolored bead necklace made by Martha's four-year-old niece. We sat at the table, surrounded by photographs of family members who had died during the holocaust.

We talked about the pilgrimage in which Martha participated. It was under the care of the Japanese Buddhist order of Nipponzan Myohoji monks who have been walking for peace in many locations of the world for decades. This is a relatively small order which organizes and leads pilgrimages for peace which are open for anyone to join for as long as the person wishes to do so.

With shaved heads, wearing saffron robes, the monks lead the pilgrimage, walking single file, chanting and beating hand-held drums. The pilgrims are hosted by churches, Quaker meetings, and other places where they are given food and a place to sleep, often on the floor.

I had the opportunity to stay overnight with these monks in Hiroshima on Hiroshima Day in 1982. In the early morning hours before dawn we chanted for what seemed like hours the words to the Odaimoku, "Na - mu - myo - ho -ren - ge - kyo" to the rhythm of the beat on a huge bass drum. The meaning of this chant was told to Martha as an affirmation:

> *Trust and peace are the values of time yet to be fully uncovered. This is our task now and in the century to come.*

The founder and leader of the order, Nichidatsu Fujii, was 98 years old at the time. He very kind and courteous to me during an interview and later presented me with a well-used hand-held drum. He told me, "We cannot continue living for the day within the next twenty years on which we will be annihilated. We must be able to live embracing a future with hope and joy."

In Beating Celestial Drums *(p. 49), Nichidatsu Fujii wrote:*

The single act of beating the drum and chanting the Odaimoku penetrates deeply into the minds and hearts of the people. This power is now exerting influence throughout the world. People shall come to acknowledge those who beat the drum and walk as central figures in the effort to create peace in the world.

Numbers on Her Father's Arm

For Martha, the ground was tilled before she was born. The experiences of her parents were so traumatic that they could never be forgotten. They permeated her childhood. A seed was planted very early in her young soul, a seed of wrestling with her own responsibility in a violent world.

Says Martha:

It began with something that I grapple with all my life. I had an awareness in my early childhood of the numbers on my father's left forearm. 1-0-8-2-6-8 are probably the first numbers in my consciousness. At age three or four, I asked him, "Who put them there?" We have no grandparents. Extended family is sparse and distant. My mother shrieks in her sleep. Everyone is dead. I asked my father, "Why did the world let it happen?" I remember how my father shrugged and said, "The world is largely indifferent to the suffering of others."

Martha does not accept that the world is indifferent. She recalls how her parents were quick to join the outcry against military intervention in Viet Nam. She remembers them speaking out against the production of arms. "My father explained, 'If you produce arms, you create a need to use them. Violence begets violence.' " She remembers that ever since she was a small child she has felt a responsibility to do what she can. She has wrestled long and hard with the question: "What is my responsibility in my own time?"

"Osweicim"

An answer to this question came to her one day in her early forties. Martha is a Quaker, a member of Cambridge Friends Meeting. One day after meeting she spotted a poster announcing a peace pilgrimage beginning in Osweicim. This word leapt out at Martha because "Osweicim" is the Polish name for the town where the Germans established the death camp, Auschwitz. Martha immediately felt called to participate. She told her friends, "I have not been able to distract myself from this initiative. It resonates deeply within me."

The Interfaith Pilgrimage for Peace and Life was sponsored by the Nipponzan Myohoji Buddhist monks from Japan. The Pilgrimage would begin with a December fast and vigil in Auschwitz-Birkenau in December of 1994. From there the pilgrims would walk prayerfully through many of the trouble spots of the world during the fiftieth anniversary year of the end of World War II. The pilgrimage was to last nine months, ending in Hiroshima and Nagasaki in August. Martha participated in the European and Middle East sections.

Finding Support

Martha talked with another Cambridge Meeting Friend who had felt called to go on the pilgrimage and had posted the notice about it. The two of them began a clearness process with Friends in the meeting. Neither of them had enough money to make the pilgrimage so they applied for grants and pooled their resources. Four people served on a support committee for Martha, helping her raise funds and keeping in touch with her by letter during the pilgrimage. Martha comments that she never could have gone on the pilgrimage without the support of her Friends Meeting community. She was held in prayer by members of her meeting community as well as by members of the fund's board after she received a grant.

Martha describes how a leading makes itself known to her. She feels it like a "tickling." She says, "A leading begins by asking, by asking God, by asking others, and by slowly gathering support." One member of her support committee walked a full day with Martha as practice. That experience helped Martha to set aside some of her fears. So much was unknown. Martha only knew she was to go.

Martha wrote a letter to friends in order to raise money:

> I face this pilgrimage with trepidation. Yet I feel my body must stand with my heart that has grieved the violence that decimated my own family. I am seeking a way to do something about what I abhor. I feel impelled to seek means to participate in this pilgrimage, prayerful that I'm being used for a purpose I don't fully apprehend. I am confident participation in the pilgrimage will inform the ministries I am called to forever after.

Poland

Even before the pilgrimage officially began, Martha and Stella had their own pilgrimage. (Victor did not wish to be part of this trip.) Stella and Martha visited Stella's home village, the first time Stella had returned since the inhabitants were murdered. They found a rough hewn stone slab, lost from public view down a labyrinth of back streets, with the words (translated into English): "5,000 Jews . . . 19 August 1942 . . . murdered in the time of Hitler terror." Stella and Martha buried a copy of the minute (a letter from Cambridge Friends Meeting) in the place that commemorates the massacre of Stella's grandparents and others.

Martha writes:

> Just after Thanksgiving, a lifetime of longing to see for myself my parents' origins is fulfilled: the birch forests; the pine forests; the filigree woodworking on cottages; the gracefulness of Cracow, my father's hometown. No wonder his implacable sense of loss. I am plunged into the culture of the first language of my consciousness. I am enchanted. Yet I know my mother must be seeing specters. She doesn't explain much; shadows pass through her eyes. She says she feels like Rip Van Winkle.

As they pass a bookstore, Martha notices a book in the window: *Czy ja jestem morderca? (Am I a Murderer?)* Martha sees it is an eyewitness account of the destruction of the Jewish population in her mother's hometown. Her mother is emphatic about not buying it. Martha comments: "Too painful? Pandora's box? I respect her wishes though I covet any shred of family history."

Months later, Martha finds the book translated into French. Martha can read French and she buys the book. Inside she finds a tribute to her mother's aunt's husband:

> He perished at Treblinka with his wife and son rather than save his own skin. You saved the honor of the Jews at Otwock. You sweetened the last moments of your wife's life.

She took this book home to her mother and father after the pilgrimage. Her mother read the words, said nothing, and marked the place with a salvaged photo of the couple.

Pilgrimage for Peace and Life

After Martha and Stella's private pilgrimage, Stella returned home and Martha joined the sixty pilgrims at Auschwitz-Birkenau for fasting and prayer. Martha wrote in her journal, "Can I ever sit on the toilet again without counting the ten seconds allocated prisoners?" From Auschwitz-Birkenau, the pilgrims followed the route of the forced march from Auschwitz-Birkenau which her father and the other prisoners walked in January 1944. Martha wrote:

> My father remembers this town. He and other camp prisoners trudged through deep snow and merciless cold, five prisoners abreast. Over three days, they were marched on to Cieszyn. No rations. No shelter. At Cieszyn, they were loaded in cattle cars that arrived at Mauthausen Concentration Camp west of Vienna five days later.

The pilgrims walked in single file with the Buddhist monks leading the way, beating their hand-held drums and chanting, "Na - mu - myo - ho -ren -ge - kyo." The group was received with unfailing hospitality in every town, given dinner and space to lay out sleeping bags on church floors.

Martha recalls, "our bones were aching because most of us were unaccustomed to walking day after day, kilometer after kilometer."

> We were mindful that we were walking with many people in our hearts. It was a privilege, being released for a time of prayer. I remember saying (to another pilgrim), "This is a time in our lives where the only obligation is to pray. That is our only duty, our only purpose, the only thing we have to do today."

Many people who have spent time on peace marches have reported the deep value of this extended time of prayer. Martha was very grateful for this aspect of the pilgrimage.

The journey was not without risk. The monks planned to walk through the most troubled spots of the world. The pilgrims went to Mostar, in former Yugoslavia, where they fasted and prayed. They were unable to get into Serbia. Martha wrote:

> The border guards (at the Serbian border) had a very menacing manner and held me and four others in detention for about five hours without explanation. They only said, we are not welcome. We were put back on the train and locked in a compartment until the Hungarian border.
>
> My heart is raw from the grief and grievance we've witnessed. I am humbled by these travels. Maybe this is their purpose. Unless I find compassion for those I reflexively condemn, I become part of an ever-escalating antagonism. No reconciliation comes through accusation. It requires, however, admitting wrongs, asking forgiveness, and making reparation.

The pilgrims often sleep on concrete floors of churches. Irritations arise. Martha writes about the difficulties of communal life.

> Step by Step, and here we are. We all fall dog tired into bed after a splash bath and scrubbing dusty socks and looking after the protestations of the digestion. I look down at my dusty, battered feet. My toes have changed shape. Our white socks are shades of gray and black no scrubbing can dissolve.
>
> It is already clear that we're challenged to live amongst ourselves the peace we proclaim audaciously to others. We are not permitted sanctimony. In a group, enmities ignite. I don't know always why they begin—as much from an irritation with oneself—as much from misunderstanding. We puzzle over it. Styles clash. Alliances form. Reconciliation is a fine art.

Martha writes:

> Can this pilgrimage save the world? Unlikely. Many
> may wonder what value there is in simply walking,
> honoring, and praying. Surely more value than sitting
> back and detachedly deploring the 6:00 p.m. news.
> We never know whose hearts are touched. In every
> case, always our own. During the war, my mother
> recalls they felt terribly abandoned by the world. I
> can not. We can not.

Celebration of Fifty Years Since
Prison Camp Liberation

After walking with the monks from December until April,
1995, Martha chose to return to Europe at the invitation of
two pilgrimage participants, one German and one Austrian,
to attend celebrations marking fifty years since the liberation of the prison camps. The three women attended the
commemoration at Dachau, near Munich, Germany. One
of these women arranged for Martha to be at the site
where her father was liberated, Gunskirchen, a satellite camp
of Mauthausen near Vienna, Austria. Martha comments:
"These valiant women are active today in not allowing the
past to be forgotten as we grapple to live humanely in our
own day."

Martha writes:

> As we arrive, I cry. The forest is innocent. It's hard to
> conceive of 18,000 people in an area smaller than
> an American supermarket. There were seven wooden
> barracks with 2,700 prisoners packed in each. Twenty
> holes in the ground for latrines. I imagine my father
> here at age 26.

Martha writes about attending the ceremony at
Mauthausen:

> I attend the official ceremony. It is mobbed. The camp in its stone massiveness presides over a fecund valley like a castle. Former prisoners file into the Appelliplatz to a brass band arrangement of Chopin's "Marche Funebre." Many are wearing scraps of their old uniforms. They identify themselves by number.
>
> I weep with admiration for the contingents of Austrians, Germans, Italians, and Spaniards, dissidents in their homelands, antifascists. I weep for "J's"— Jugoslawens. Though they suffered together here, today they live in warring countries and walk under separate flags: Bosnia, Croatia, Slovenia, Yugoslavia. Over the public address system, a former inmate recalls the camaraderie of those dreadful days. He pleads for universal brotherhood.

At the end of the afternoon, Martha reads the newspaper headlines about massacres in Rwanda, a report of a Palestinian man shaken to death while in Israeli custody, and the resumption of fighting in Croatia. Martha asks the question that continues to haunt her, "What is my responsibility in my own time?"

Looking Back

As I interview Martha three years later, we talk about the effect of going on this pilgrimage. She is very grateful for the experience.

> I was extraordinarily privileged. It was through the love and support of so many people. It made connections for me. It pushed me into the world again. It gave me community. I guess as an act of faith I have to believe that I am on my way, that I continue to do my best to act in faithfulness.

She remarks:

> The pilgrimage was precious beyond all telling in in-
> effable ways for me personally. What the meaning is
> to me has yet to unfold. The responsibility that I feel
> for the trust that people placed in me will carry
> through my whole life, not the least of which was
> going to the places of my parents' origin.

One of the best aspects of the pilgrimage, Martha thinks,
was the community that was formed among the walkers
themselves. It offered the participants a chance to meet and
get to know other like-minded people, people who were willing to physically make a journey for peace. Martha has continued to keep in touch with these friends.

Martha read an account by a man who was liberated from
Buchenwald in April of 1945 who commented that one of
the meanings of that horrific experience for him is that there
is redemption in camaraderie. Martha resonates with that
insight, saying, "For me, therein lies the supreme, sublime
meaning. As much as human community has its treachery,
it also has its sublimity. And in our love for one another, in
our searching to make life on earth together, yes, we can
betray, but yes, we can ennoble. We have to keep working
together to be accountable and to be held accountable. We
get lost and we find our way."

What Now?

Three years later Martha works as a high school teacher in
Slovenia, part of former Yugoslavia bordering Italy, Croatia,
Hungary, and Austria. She explains her hunger to be in that
part of the globe. She says, "Were it not for an accident of
history, I might have been raised in that world."

Martha feels that going on the original Pilgrimage for Peace
and Life was the springboard for her teaching in Slovenia

today. "I don't think I would have had the strength to live abroad if it weren't for that pilgrimage," she says. "It renewed my world citizenship."

One reason poetry has a special place in Martha's heart is because her father likes to tell the story of how poetry saved his life. When Victor was a prisoner in Auschwitz camp, he learned there was a job open at the infirmary. To work there was a privileged position. You had better food, better medicine, and lighter work to do. Many prisoners applied for the job. The job was to keep records, so the doctor wanted to test Victor's reading ability. To test him, Victor was asked to read Schiller's poem "Die Gloche" (The Bell—a famous poem of freedom against tyranny). Victor knew that poem by heart and recited it. Because he was able to recite poetry, Victor got the job in the infirmary.

Nudges from God

Martha continues to seek information related to her family roots in Poland. During her vacation times she is often drawn towards Germany and Poland. While she continually listens for the guidance from God, she is often surprised by what God leads her to do. She comments, "My experience of God is never what I anticipate . . . never." Martha repeats a joke a pilgrimage colleague told her: "How do you make God laugh?" Answer: "You tell her your plans."

Last year Martha visited a German friend, Heidrun. This woman had been a little girl during the war years. Just before the trip to Germany, Martha picked up a tiny book on the Holocaust to read on the train. Martha says:

> It felt as if dear old God were saying to me, "Martha, don't forget, you cannot forget this reality of things, the draconian reality of things. You are going to Germany and as much as you would like to be a proper

guest and not stir up these specters, that is part of who you are and it is important not to forget.

Although Martha had not been aware of it at the time she planned the trip, Martha's visit to Munich (where her parents were married) happened to coincide with her parents' fiftieth wedding anniversary. After she got there she realized how this was an answer to her prayers. She had been thinking and praying about how she could help refugees. In her own mind this was Bosnian refugees. But here she was in Munich making a pilgrimage to the place where her parents had been refugees. Heidrun made the pilgrimage with her, finding the place where Martha's parents had their first apartment and the location of the city hall in which they were married.

> My visit with Heidrun gave me a sense that the world can and does heal. Heidrun and I have an extraordinary and tender bond. What is rent in one generation is mended in the next by some miracle, some spirit of life that is best not to try to put in a box. God is unconventional. To try not to judge God or anticipate God, those are disciplines.

Martha repeated for emphasis, "Those are the disciplines. This I know experimentally."

Return to Poland

Last fall Martha returned to Stella's home town, the place of the massacre, the place where she first went with Stella in 1994. The idea to go began in Slovenia when Martha heard a whispering in her ear, "Come back, come back." She felt drawn to return to that place of massacre. When she told her parents, her parents were anxious. They urged her not to go back to Poland. She was warned by other people as well that it might be dangerous to go to Poland because of her Jewish background. "There are such echoes of anguish there," she says, "hostility towards Jews." In spite of these warnings Martha felt compelled to follow her leading to make this journey. She said, "I feel that this is a work of reconciliation, the difficult, delicate work of reconciliation." Martha was not sure she could find the way to the memorial, but she followed the paths she remembered taking with her mother three years ago. She found the stone that marks the massacre of her mother's home town. "I was afraid, I confess," she says. "I stood at the grave site and wondered, would I be met with hostility?"

At that moment a group of little children came with their school teacher and lit candles there. It was All-Soul's Day (November 1), the time to remember the dead. Martha was overwhelmed. She says, "My lamentation turned to joy."

Martha had a photograph of her grandmother and grandfather and showed it to the children and their teacher. Martha pointed to the photo and said the German words for grandmother and grandfather. The children and their teacher understood. The little group posed for a photograph for Martha to take home. When Martha had come with her mother in 1994 she had not had a good camera, so she wanted to document this trip for her family.

The teacher invited Martha to come to the school and have tea. "Herbata." The children lighting the candles and the friendship of the teacher made this a special day of reconciliation for Martha.

Each of these mini-pilgrimages has been important to Martha. Each one expands Martha's connections to her own roots. Now she has mental images of the places where her family members were killed. Although it is painful to be there, it is also fulfilling a deep yearning for Martha. In each journey there have been blessings, adding good memories to the painful ones.

Loneliness

Although she is having many meaningful experiences, Martha is lonely. She has been living away from family and home for several years. Ever since she went on the Pilgrimage for Peace and Life she has been living overseas. She confesses, "I am homesick."

"Was Thee Faithful?"

As Martha reflects on pilgrimages she has taken, she says:

> Pilgrimage is an offering, a gesture to God of my own willingness to be remade. It is God's invitation to give one more piece of the puzzle. All I can offer is my own stupidity, my own brokenness, my own asking questions, my own confession that I don't know. But I have these skills. I have this heart.

The hardest part of the Pilgrimage for Peace and Life was learning that there is no magic wand. Martha comments:

> Wouldn't it be nice if by our walking we had put an end to war. Maybe it is a bit childish to confess but that is one of the hardest parts, to accept that the questions don't have any answers in any absolute way, that we have to continue to pose the questions and continue to try to answer them. Question and confession in the fullest sense of the word. Questions remain and we have to respond because we are God's hands and feet and ears and legs. We must be willing to hear the answers and keep the fingers out of our ears when we are prompted. There is that wonderful Quaker query: "Was thee faithful?"

IX. THE STRUGGLE FOR JUSTICE

Elaine Bishop

Elaine Bishop

He has showed you, O man, what is good.
And what does the Lord require of you?
To act justly and to love mercy
and to walk humbly with your God.

Micah 6:6 (NIV)

E laine Bishop lived for four years in Little Buffalo, the community for the Lubicon Cree people of Canada. She was led to go there to join the Lubicon, one of the aboriginal peoples of Canada, in their struggle to regain their Aboriginal land rights.

Elaine is living at a Quaker Center, Woodbrooke, in England after her years in Little Buffalo with the Lubicon people. It has been a full year since Elaine left Little Buffalo and moved to the United Kingdom. She leads me upstairs to her small, bright room. On the walls of her room are pictures of her mother and many of her friends. This quote by St. Teresa of Avila is pinned up (Elaine had penciled in "and women" after the word "men" in the last line.)

> Christ has no body on earth but yours.
> No feet but yours.
> Yours are the eyes through which must look out
> Christ's compassion on the world.
> Yours are the feet with which He is to go about doing good.
> Yours are the hands with which He is to bless men now.

Elaine is of medium stature, with long brown hair, and is dressed informally in tee shirt and jeans. She speaks in a "down-to-earth" way, with openness and great honesty. What is most striking is the passionate way she speaks about the land rights issues that plague the aboriginal peoples of Canada. For most of her adult life she has been actively involved in working alongside others to bring about conditions for peace and justice. Elaine served as Coordinator of Canadian Friends Service Committee, Clerk of Canadian Yearly Meeting, and Chairperson of the Aboriginal Rights Coalition (an ecumenical church coalition).

The social concerns which lead Quakers such as Elaine into social and political activism have their roots in Quaker beliefs and testimonies. In Faith and Practice of New England Yearly Meeting of Friends (pp. 173-174), Dorothy H. Hutchinson, a twentieth-century Friend, writes:

The basis of Friends' social concern is the same as the basis of Quakerism as a whole —the belief in the within-ness of God. This is not original with Friends. Many other groups have believed that God is within as well as above and beyond man. However, the emphasis on the within-ness of God in all human beings, in the capacity of the individual to communicate directly with God, to experience the spirit of Christ and express it in every aspect of life has led us to adopt patterns of behavior which may be considered distinctively Quaker.

This is the spiritual basis of the Friends' distinctive form of meeting for worship — waiting in the Light for direct revelation of God's will for us. It is the basis for the distinctive form of meeting for business —seeking unity in the Spirit. And it is the basis for all the social testimonies.

The concern arises as a revelation to an individual that there is a painful discrepancy between existing social conditions and what God wills for society and that this discrepancy is not being adequately dealt with. The next step is the determination of the individual to do something about it —not because he is particularly well fitted to tackle the problem, but simply because no one else seems to be doing it.

In the following story, Elaine Bishop has a concern for justice. Her concern arises as she observes what she perceives to be oppression by the Canadian government in refusing to observe the land rights of indigenous Lubicon people of northern Alberta. She makes the decision to go to live with these people for a time in the hopes that she may learn more about the situation and be of some service to them in their struggle for justice.

Forty-nine years old at the time of the interview, Elaine is in a time of transition, a time of reflection on the past and preparation for whatever God leads her to do in the future. She is waiting on God.

Background

After we sat in prayerful silence for a few minutes, Elaine spoke about her childhood in Canada.

> I can't remember a time in which God was not present in my life in some way. And always I had a concern around justice, as long as I can remember. As a small child I remember asking questions like, "Why is there poverty?" "Why is there war?" That does not make sense to me.
>
> One of the things Mum was involved in, the Voice of Women, was a women's peace group. On Mother's Day they would celebrate by holding a twenty-four hour vigil for peace on the corner of Portage and Main, the windiest corner in Winnipeg, Manitoba. I would go down there.
>
> So my memory of growing up was Mother's Day peace vigils and Red Cross club in the school which was the closest thing to social justice. I was volunteering in the hospital. I was not too interested in dating, probably because there were not too many young men who were as passionate as I was about the things I was passionate about. My world was always big enough to include the fact that I knew that there was injustice around the world and just to allow it to be and not to do anything about it did not make any sense.

Health has been a continual concern. Throughout her life Elaine has lived with chronic illness, a mild form of systemic lupus. When she has flair-ups she experiences profound exhaustion, much joint pain, and even kidney problems.

Elaine earned a Master's in social work in her twenties. She worked in battered women's shelters and worked for the abolition of prisons through the Quaker Committee on Jails and Justice. At the age of thirty-nine, she became co-ordinator for Canadian Friends Service Committee at the office in Toronto. As part of this work, she became chairperson of Aboriginal Rights Coalition in 1988. It is typical for Elaine to be given the leadership role. She admits her ability freely, and yet does not seem to have any ego about it. She simply says, with a laugh:

> The thing is I am good at it, and I don't tolerate it very well when it is done badly. I admit it is some-times easier to put the extra work in and make it go well.

It was her work with the aboriginal peoples of Canada that eventually led to spending four years with the Lubicon in Little Buffalo.

Background of the Lubicon Land Claim

The Lubicon have been struggling for their land rights ever since white people came into the territory. This territory, about four thousand square miles, is in what is now north-ern Alberta.

Elaine offers a brief summary of the history of the land rights issue: In 1899 and 1900, a huge land transfer took place with the signing of Treaty 8. The government wanted access to the land for settlement and resource extraction. By the time the treaty was made, many of the aboriginal peoples (known as First Nations) were facing profound threats to their territories. First of all they were dying of illnesses brought in by Europeans, to which they had no immunity. Secondly, an influx of settlers wanted land for farming or ranching.

Treaty 8 Commissioners traveled during the summers of 1899 and 1900 with translators, and often with priests. They tried to get First Nations to sign the treaty. Elaine points out that the concepts implicit in the treaties—that the land could be given up and that their rights as First Nations could be "extinguished"—did not exist within the languages of these peoples.

The crucial point is this: The Lubicon were not contacted by the treaty commissioners at that time they were on the land between the rivers. The Lubicon never signed Treaty 8. Yet the governments of Canada and Alberta have not respected this fact and have claimed that the Treaty 8 blankets the Lubicon territory. In the 1930s the land was transferred, by Canadian government authority, into Alberta jurisdiction. In 1939 the Lubicon registered as a "band" and were promised a treaty and a reserve. The survey for the reserve was never completed, however, and the treaty was never signed.

In the 1950s, under the Lubicon territory, oil extraction began and has grown slowly over the years. Thirty years later, in 1980, the first all-weather road into this territory was completed and oil extraction escalated. The Lubicon consider this to be unlawful intrusion into their territory.

In the 1970s and 1980s, the Lubicon tried for twelve years to find a court that would adjudicate its conflict. Governmental legal tactics prevented the issues from coming to court. The Lubicon filed a complaint under the United Nations. The UN recognized that the Lubicon had not been able to get justice through the systems in Canada. The UN directed Canada to take no further action that might endanger the Lubicon and to resolve the dispute.

That dispute still has not been resolved. In 1987, to make matters worse, the provincial government made an agreement with a multi-national pulp company, giving it the right to harvest every tree on Lubicon territory. Says Elaine, "The Lubicon oppose this, seeing clear cutting as murder of the environment."

Until about 1980, the community of Lubicon people was self-supporting. Escalating resource extraction has destroyed the ecological balance of the territory, however, and the number of game has plummeted. The community has become welfare dependent. English as the language of instruction in the school and the language of the invasive electronic media threatens the minority Lubicon language and culture.

The next chapter came in 1988 when the Lubicon engaged in major public education and non-violent resistance focusing on the Olympic Games held in Calgary. Some of the oil companies extracting resources from the Lubicon territory sponsored a museum exhibition of Aboriginal artifacts. The Lubicon instigated a museum boycott of this exhibit and staged demonstrations along the Canada-wide Olympic flame run.

In her position as chairperson of the Aboriginal Rights Coalition, Elaine was actively engaged in supporting the Lubicon. In the summer of 1988, the Lubicon Chief and an Elder spoke at Canadian Yearly Meeting of Friends. These Quakers were deeply moved and responded by appointing a delegation to stand with the Lubicon in their struggle for land rights.

That year, 1988, the Lubicon withdrew from the courts and asserted jurisdiction, once again, over their traditional territory, putting up barricades. Elaine was one of three representatives of Canadian Yearly Meeting sent to stand with the Lubicon during this action.

Elaine recalls:

> This was my first trip to Lubicon territory. Five days after the assertion of jurisdiction started, the Royal Canadian Mounted Police, armed with an ex parte injunction, moved in with over 200 officers, armed with dogs, shot guns, and SWAT team members. They arrested twenty-seven people and took down the barricades. After a day in jail we were released. Two days later the Chief negotiated a settlement with the

Provincial Premier, however the federal government, which is the government responsible for resolving Aboriginal land rights disputes, never agreed to this settlement.

A Nudge to Move On

Gradually Elaine began to feel God leading her to be more closely involved, to go and live with the Lubicon and to do what she could to support their struggle. She went through a great deal of personal discernment as she wrestled with leaving her job at Canadian Friends Service Committee and moving in this direction. She experienced an on-going process of struggle to accept the leading.

When a person is discerning a leading, it often takes a long time. The leading may grow very slowly inside a person, like a plant beginning to grow, yet invisible still below the surface of the earth. Then at some point in time something will trigger a shift, there will be a moment of clarity, and the leading will be out there, above the earth in the light of day for all to see.

It was at an Assembly of the Dene, one of the First Nations of Canada, in what is known as British Colombia, that Elaine felt such a shift. Elaine wrote about it to her friends:

> It was my first experience of being far enough north that the sky did not become dark in the summer. I had a wonderful time! The land is beautiful and strong. The Assembly was moving as each chief spoke about the struggles of her or his community, many accessible only by water or air. Deep concerns were expressed about damage done to the environment by pollution, about the land claim, about ways of being Dene in a modern world.
>
> The Seminar ended with a day of silence and fasting on the land. I camped for this day beside a

small waterfall. About 11:30 at night I went for a walk and as I returned to my tent I found the tops of the coniferous trees bathed in gold as the sun dipped below the horizon. Amazing beyond words!

It was during this retreat that Elaine became clear to quit her job. She wrote:

I have been with Canadian Friends Service Committee for almost three and a half years. I took the job as a result of a leading. It has clearly been a right place for me and for the Yearly Meeting.

My spiritual life has grown tremendously during this time. I have been challenged by the level of destruction and damage I see on a daily basis as we work for social justice. My work with First Nations, with their special relationship to the earth, has been a growing edge for me over the past four years. I have found that native spirituality has enriched my own journey.

Over the past year, though, I have had a growing sense of change. I have found it harder to live in a large city, where there is no silence. I have wanted to have some ground in which to plant growing things. I also have had a growing sense of wanting children to be part of my life. I have explored this growing sense of dis-ease with my committee of care and with the Friend whom I consider a spiritual guide. I have received support to search further this sense of needing to change.

I have worked for the last three and a half years in international development and aboriginal justice. Now the sense was a calling to work with a smaller focus, in a place north and west of where I am now, but without knowing where that will be. The sense at this time is to prepare for this next phase.

Where Will I Get the Money?

To quit her job was the first step. But then she would be left with where to get the money to support her leading. Elaine was leaving a good job and moving into the unknown. She had no private savings to support herself. She did not know where she could find financial support. This is often true of people who continue to follow the leadings they believe God is giving them. They must step off the cliff and have faith that they will not crash into the abyss, that they will not starve, that they will be given what they need. This can be one of the scariest parts of surrendering to God's guidance. This is a continuing issue Elaine has had to face.

Elaine was aware that leaving paid employment in a recession may not seem good "economic" sense, but she had a sense of rightness about it. She began to plan for a year of teacher training in preparation for finding a job among the indigenous people of Northern Canada.

Taking a Break

First, Elaine took a break. She was wise enough to realize she could not go straight from an intense full-time job into the next job. She knew she needed a rest, a time of integration, and preparation. She was fortunate to be able to spend three months at the Quaker center, Pendle Hill, resting, studying liberation theology and scripture, and reflecting on some of her experiences.

One experience from the year before kept coming to her mind. She had been at an ecumenical consultation on "Partnership in the 1990s" in which eight church denominations had each brought representative "partners" from the economically-deprived world with whom they worked. Elaine remembers, "The participants from the economically-deprived world were very gentle but very clear with us." They asked, "Are you ready to give up your privilege so that our people have a chance to live?" This became a central query for Elaine at Pendle Hill.

At Pendle Hill Elaine spent time discerning God's leading for her. She wrote:

> The theme that has woven through my spiritual journey over the past ten years has been the sense of accepting leadings and following them even if the way of doing so is not always clear. My experience has been that I am given what I need to know to get to the next stage. As I am faithful things become clear. I have become much more grounded and feel blessed beyond words! So it does not surprise me that the leading at this point only goes as far as knowing that I need to complete the year of teacher training. None of which relieves me of the task of finding ways to enable this to happen! Rather I am able to go about searching with a sense of somewhat awed confidence, after seeking clearness that the way is right.

Elaine wrote that letter when she was feeling "up." And yet, in her heart of hearts, there continued to be pockets of doubt and fear. After all, she still did not know where she would be going. Even after she was well into the Bachelor of Education, the teacher training course in preparation for going to live with aboriginal peoples, she was still experiencing difficulty accepting her leading. Her journal was full of discouragement and even deep depression. She needed to keep her faith that God was guiding her. Elaine admits, "I have feet of clay." Yet she felt drawn to live with the Lubicon. All she could do was try to live as much in the Light as possible. She recalls, "It was a time of living on a knife edge."

When Elaine applied for a job as a teacher in the Northland School Division in Alberta, where the Lubicon Cree people live, she was told that Northland was not hiring people from outside Alberta that year. After quitting her job and taking a year of teacher training, the job was not available. Elaine then contacted a Mennonite colleague to inquire about working in that region for the Mennonite's Volunteer Service Program. This colleague visited the Lubicon and found out they would welcome Elaine as a volunteer. The Mennonite Central Committee agreed to accept her into its Volunteer Service Program, giving her basic funding, support, and supervision. She was to work as an educational coordinator, helping the community address issues around education.

Tried by Storm and Fire

Elaine moved to Little Buffalo in July of 1992. After she had been there ten days a teaching position opened up at the school, for which she was invited to apply. Elaine responded that she had already found a position under the Mennonites. Her Mennonite supervisor was visiting at the time and urged her to take the job in the school. The Chief agreed.

Elaine recalls:

> My immediate gut response was "This is the wrong thing for me to be doing." But my directions from my two key supervisors were to take the position. It was a quick discussion. Neither of them said to me, "Do you think this is the right thing to do?" They just said, "Go for it," and my stomach went "Kuh."

So Elaine applied for and got the job and attended the orientation for new teachers in August. She says:

> Within four days I knew it was absolutely the wrong thing for me to be doing. I couldn't think. I felt like I was doing a terrible job. It felt absolutely a profound wrong. Then we had a long weekend. I couldn't work; I couldn't think; I couldn't organize. All of those are things I can do really well.

So she called her provincial Mennonite supervisor (not the person who encouraged her to take the job). "I cried a lot on the phone," she says. "I told her, 'I can't do this.'" The woman understood and agreed to support her decision to leave the school job. Elaine says:

> I had to go tell the Chief and it was a terribly hard thing to do. And I had to tell the head of the Indigenous local school board. I had to break a contract that I had signed, something I had never had to do before. All of this was incredibly hard. I'm not used to quitting, so then there were all sorts of questions about my sense of self-image.

Elaine continues:

> As I was processing this, it became quite clear to me that the reason I couldn't do it was: As a teacher I would be expected to teach the children the culture that was destroying their culture. I felt that would be a betrayal to them.

She reports, "The Chief was not surprised. He had not thought I would be able to stick the school."

Other people in the community told her, "Now you know what our kids go through." There was already a bond between Elaine and the community because she went to jail with them in 1988 as a representative of Quakers. She had been through the fire with them. This time people accepted her in a profoundly different way.

She recalls, "People would come up to me and say, 'I hear you quit the school.'"

"And I would say, 'Yep.'"

"And they would say, 'How come?'"

"And I would say, 'I'm not prepared to teach your kids how to be white.'"

"And they would say, 'Yep.'"

"And that was all that would be said," says Elaine, "but things changed in terms of relationship. That was a real tempering process. I really felt like I had been tried by the fire and it took awhile to get my confidence back."

Elaine comments:

> So in terms of following a leading, it doesn't mean it
> is going to be easy; it doesn't mean you are not go-
> ing to be tried by storm and fire. There may be such
> a thing as an easy leading, but I don't think so.

She laughs. "Yet it was profoundly important to have that
experience. I learned a heck of a lot about colonialism in a
short period of time. I could not have learned this any
other way."

What Did You Do There?

While the teachers at the school lived in special housing
with inside bathrooms, Elaine chose to live under the same
conditions as the Lubicon. She wrote:

> My day starts with stoking up the wood stove before
> the walk to the outhouse. This is a community with-
> out running water so all but the teachers share this
> experience. I chop my own wood and usually spend
> part of the day visiting and part with local children
> coming in and hanging out here.

The community work Elaine did in Little Buffalo was a
response to a request from the Chief or from other community members. As a Mennonite Volunteer Service person,
she was expected to offer "presence ministry." This
means responding to needs that arise in the community,
which turned out to be inviting the children to use her home
as a play center, driving folk to the hospital, and whatever
came up.

One job was to be an informal liaison with the school and
with other educational institutions. Young people would talk
with her about educational plans, and she would assist them
with funding and support. Elaine worked with the Women's

Circle. The Women's Circle developed a variety of activities for children: video evenings, baseball games, hot dog roasts, crafts, etc. The Circle put on workshops about alcohol abuse or how to do beading or make moccasins. Some women from the Women's Circle traveled to solidarity events as speakers. Elaine did some of the secretarial tasks like taking notes, keeping financial records, and finding sources of funding. Elaine says:

> The women really are impressive and strong. They are aware of the ways in which the land rights conflict has broken their community and are committed to work for healing.

The land rights struggle took much of her time: making presentations, helping develop strategies, and doing public education. Elaine arranged to go on speaking tours in Britain. When visitors came, Elaine would welcome them, orient them to the land rights issues, and lead tours. Elaine's communication with the outside world took time and organization because the nearest bank, post office, and stores were sixty miles away.

She wrote to friends:

> The joys are many. I am becoming friends with many wonderful people. I am learning to live in a slower, yet still full, rhythm. Children are a much more constant part of my life. I feel centered and spiritually nourished although I greatly miss a regular Quaker meeting.

How Do You Handle the Hard Parts?

One of the continuing threads of Elaine's life is that she must struggle financially. While her basic needs were met during her time in Little Buffalo (shelter, water, and wood from the community, and a subsistence level stipend from the Mennonites), Elaine did not have resources to cover program expenses. She had to write to her friends for funds to cover those expenses the first year.

It was hard for Elaine to be there and experience the oppression first hand. "I became enraged," she says. "It was MY government, and I was going to the funerals and seeing the stillbirths and seeing the damage to the land."

Elaine takes everything to God in prayer. "I scream at God at times," she says. "I have confidence that God can absorb that and continue to use me; that is one of the ways God supports me in this work."

Prayer was an essential part of the day. Elaine says:

> One of the things I have done for a long time is, I start and end my day talking to God. When I turn out the lights and lie down on the pillow I give thanks to God. At night I think about both the good and the bad things and give thanks for both. In the morning I give thanks for the morning and the potential of the day.

One meditation practice Elaine uses is a Buddhist practice, the Metabovena. It is a practice of developing loving kindness. In the Metabovena you choose three people, one person you really love, one person you feel neutral about, and third a person you are in conflict with. And you start out by picking a person and then saying, may this person (use the person's name) be well, may this person be happy, may this person be free from suffering. You start with yourself, then you go to the person you love, then the person you feel neutral towards, and then the person you feel in conflict with. Then you do the four together, may we all be well, may we all be happy, may we all be free from suffering.

Elaine likes to add "May all of humanity be well . . . happy . . . free from suffering." She includes the earth: "May the earth be well . . . happy . . . free from suffering." She includes creation: "May all of creation be well . . . be happy . . . be free from suffering." She ends up with "May God be well . . . happy . . . free from suffering." Elaine says,

"This has really been profound for me." The simplest prayer Elaine uses came from a Cree Elder who told her: "The only prayer that is needed is, 'Thanks be to God.' No matter what happens in the day, 'Thanks be to God.'"

Throughout her time in Little Buffalo Elaine journaled a lot. She recalls:

> Much of it was pretty impolite. Sometimes I got depressed. At times I would cry. It was particularly tough because I was so isolated.

Elaine points out:

> It was tough for me, but it was tougher for the community, seeing their land destroyed, their community being destroyed, and promises being made and broken. Yet they continued to struggle to create justice for their children and grandchildren."

Support

Support is a vital part of ministry. Particularly when one is working in a culture that is different from one's own, one needs support of all kinds. Some support can come from the local people among whom you work. But you also need outside support, financial, emotional, and spiritual, from your home base. Ideally people go in pairs to do this kind of ministry, so that there will be someone with whom to share experiences. Elaine was called to go alone, but she had a tremendous amount of support.

Perhaps Elaine's most crucial support came from within the community which offered her a home, wood, and access to water. Elaine relates, "When I arrived, one family took me under their wing. Their house was always open to me, and I had some of the most incredible discussions of theology with one member of the family, staying up until one a.m., followed by a walk home in minus fifty-degree temperatures, but with the northern lights dancing in the sky overhead. This family also made sure that I was supplied with water and included me in special meals and sharing of moose meat."

The nearest Friends' meeting was in Edmonton, five hundred kilometers away (about 400 miles) from Little Buffalo. Elaine transferred her membership to that meeting. A couple who were members there gave her the keys to their house and told her she could come and go as she pleased. Every two or three months, Elaine made the trip to Edmonton to go to meeting for worship.

She scheduled a solo meeting for worship in her own home at the same time as Edmonton Friends' meeting for worship. Sometimes a visitor or someone from the community joined her. One time a few of the members of the Edmonton Friends' Meeting visited Elaine in Little Buffalo.

Because there was no Friends meeting, Elaine went to the local Catholic church. She says, "I went to mass every week and, as it felt right, I celebrated communion with them."

At Peace River, the nearest town, was Brenda, the minister of the United Church. Brenda's home became a place Elaine could stay overnight when she needed a chance to get away. Her water faucets often filled Elaine's drinking water barrels that provided decent water for tea and cooking.

One man, Fred, who has been working closely with the Lubicon since the 1970s, became a good friend. Elaine and Fred often spoke daily on the telephone about developments in the struggle. Elaine comments, "Fred knew what I lived with in ways that no one else did, although a spiritual basis of life is not part of his reality."

Canadian Yearly Meeting was a tremendous support. Part of the time Elaine was in Little Buffalo she was also clerk of Canadian Yearly Meeting. This meant she had a reason, several times a year, to go and spend time with Friends. As Canadian Yearly Meeting's representative to the Aboriginal Rights Coalition, Elaine stayed in weekly telephone contact with a friend on staff there.

Every once in a while Elaine needed a total getaway. The Sisters of St. John the Divine, an Anglican women's order based in Toronto, gave Elaine an open invitation to come for retreat at their center. She took them up on it on two occasions.

Moving On

After four years, in the summer of 1996, Elaine felt it was time to move on. She comments:

> It was hard to break away. I had been invited to stay there the rest of my life. The Chief had invited me. And yet it was really clear to me that if I had stayed, it would have created more and more dependency.

Looking back on her time with the Lubicon, Elaine says that one of the hardest parts was seeing the oil companies coming into the area. Although at times she felt discouraged, the Lubicon and their supporters never gave up. Elaine remembers how they were continually devising strategies to attempt to affect the situation. She reports, "Some companies were less harmful than others, but there was certainly much destruction done while I was there." She recalls having a strong sense of frustration. She says, "Sometimes I had to watch the situation and not be able to do anything except to be present. It was tough. I was the bridge, because I knew how to deal with my culture and my government, and many Lubicon didn't. And yet we could not figure it out; not all of us."

Elaine says:

> I am not good at waiting. I am a doer. I want to go out and change the world. I can't block myself off from acknowledging the pain. I don't experience the pain the way the survivors of the oppression experience it, but I can't shut it out. This makes living in the world

a painful process. Because everywhere you go and everywhere you are, there is the pain of oppression.

Re-entry back into her own culture was a shock. She stayed for a year at Woodbrooke, a Quaker study center in England. Elaine says:

> I was just exhausted. In many ways I felt more discouraged when I came out (from Little Buffalo) than at almost any other time when I was there. I had gone through ups and downs and tough times. I was really strong with the women in the community. But I had gotten caught in some of the community tensions. Things had not been going well in the negotiations. It was really tough.

Elaine knew she was very tired and needed a rest. Her sense of frustration at the continuing injustice was painful. She says, "When I left Canada I did not want to have anything to do with Canada. I was so angry with my government." Elaine found herself with a much anger towards others and towards herself. She was fortunate to do some spiritual work with the Biblical Studies tutor at Woodbrooke, a former Jesuit priest. She says:

> My spiritual direction was around surrender and forgiveness. Partly I needed to forgive myself. Because I have been involved in aboriginal justice for over twenty years. Others have been involved in it far longer than I have. We have not figured out how to go back into our own community and enable justice to be done. To me that is a terrible indictment. I had to work on forgiving myself.

Elaine again faced financial insecurity. She wondered about her old age. She said:

> I have just come through a six-year period without setting aside any money for pension. That is the

challenge of faith. I have to believe that when I am old, the resources that I have put together will be sufficient to my needs. And it pushes me a little bit to have that faith at times.

Yet in spite of difficulties, Elaine continued to be open to the nudges from within. "The basis of my life now is (following my) leading," she says.

It is really clear to me that I am not meant to be making money or on a career path. The process of accepting the cost of that is that my belongings have been refined down. I have about twelve boxes of books and five suitcases of clothes, and that is about it. But when I see pictures of people in Calcutta where people are sleeping on the sidewalk, I think, "I'm rich."

Reflecting upon the four years she spent living with the Lubicon, Elaine says:

Through it all I received at least as much—or more— than I gave. I was welcomed, although my understanding of Lubicon Cree culture was profoundly inadequate. My attempts to learn Cree were welcomed although they were never successful. I learned at least as much about my own culture and people by seeing them through Lubicon eyes as I did about Lubicon culture and traditions. I learned a profound amount about oppression, about courage, about the value—beyond words—of the land, and of the integration of all of life in a circle of faith that surrounds and undergirds all.

X. BURNOUT AND RECOVERY

John Calvi

John Calvi

I am now remaining in and around Washington, daily visiting the hospitals. Am much in Patent-office, Eighth street, H street, Armory-square, and others. Am now able to do a little good, having money . . . and getting experience. To-day, Sunday afternoon and till nine in the evening, visited Cambell hospital; attended specially to one case in ward 1, very sick with pleurisy and typhoid fever, young man, farmer's son, D. F. Russell, company E. 60th New York, downhearted and feeble.

Walt Whitman, Specimen Days

J ohn's small, cozy bungalow lies on a beautiful wooded piece of property up a dead end country road. The home is simple, a wood stove for heat and a composting toilet. John, colorful in a bright red shirt, greets me with a big smile and a hug, inviting me into his large, comfortable living room. He has prepared leek and broccoli soup for our lunch. We sit down at the table where a vase full of purple tulips brightens up this gray winter day.

John's healing work is well known to me. For the last sixteen years John has been working with people traumatized by sexual abuse, torture, and life-threatening diseases like AIDS. John does a combination of massage, energy work, and prayer. In more recent years John has also been teaching other people about healing from trauma. One of his most popular workshops is for people in the helping professions, teaching them to avoid burnout.

Burnout can be an extremely debilitating experience related to the helping professions. In their book How Can I Help? (pp. 184-85), Ram Dass and Paul Gorman describe it this way:

> Mutual support feels most right when it's like passing around helpings of food at the table. It's all very spontaneous. One gesture follows another. There's little self-consciousness about asking and offering. And everyone gets fed. Yet most of the time we're not all sitting around together passing out helpings. Circumstance prevents us from making it to the same table at the same time. We can't always wait for that feeling of sweetness and spontaneity from which generosity flows so easily. When help is needed, it's needed. Someone's in trouble right now. Whether or not our heart is open or our mind is at rest, something has to be done.
>
> Much of the time we're able to adjust to these conditions. But at certain points—whether as the result

of circumstances or the unexpected consequence of choice—helping out gets heavy. The care of others starts to be real work. A growing burden of personal responsibility leads to exhaustion and frustration. We feel as if we're putting out more than we're getting back. And are we making any difference anyway? We're tired of being with needy people, and embarrassed or guilty about feeling that way. As our heart begins to close down, joy and inspiration give way to apathy and resignation. There arises a range of emotions and responses we've come to call burnout.

As our society has become increasingly reliant on the work of helping professionals, more and more attention has been given to the constellation of experiences we refer to as burnout. . . . Nothing may be more important, in all this, than being gentle with ourselves. Whether we're professionals working a sixty-hour week or simply family members called upon to care daily for a sick relative, facing suffering continuously is no small task. We learn the value of recognizing our limits, forgiving ourselves our bouts of impatience or guilt, acknowledging our own needs. We see that to have compassion for others we must have compassion for ourselves.

In the following story, John Calvi is led into a very demanding life-calling of working as a massage therapist, offering treatments to AIDS patients and victims of torture and other abuse. Eventually the intensity of this work becomes overwhelming, causing burnout. John describes how it happened to him and what steps he took to deal with it. Since then he has made a study of burnout and learned some ways to prevent it. John leads workshops for caregivers on this topic.

How It All Began

It was the AIDS epidemic that propelled John into spiritual transformation and a life of service. "It was terrifying, absolutely terrifying," says John, remembering what was going on in Colorado in the early 1980s. "No one knew whether or not AIDS was a virus," recalls John.

> No one knew what symptoms to look for until a person was very sick with it. Sick people were terrified to come forward until they had to.

At that time John was in his early thirties and had just finished training at massage school. He was hoping to get a job as a masseur on a cruise ship and was visualizing a comfortable life working on a luxury liner in a warm climate, playing his guitar and singing for the guests at night.

But that was not to be. Other plans were brewing for John. The first thing that happened to John was one of his massages triggered a dramatic healing for a woman. This woman who had been having trouble keeping food down was advised by her doctor to go for a massage. The doctor thought it might relax her. John recalls:

> In the midst of this session my hands got very warm. This woman began to shake and cry. At that time she regained the memory of having been abducted and tortured.

This was the beginning of a major healing for this woman.

John was amazed and puzzled. This kind of experience was not covered in his massage training. He wondered, "What is going on?"

The woman told her friends and the word got out. Other women who were suffering from childhood and adult sexual abuse came to John for massage. Over and over these women experienced release from emotional and physical pain.

John could not understand what was happening. Using his rational mind, John thought about his years working as a preschool teacher, learning to create safe space for children. Could being in a safe space enable healing to happen? John wondered.

As this happened over and over again, his hands getting hot and his clients' pain diminishing, John relates, "I began to realize that it was something more than me being nice." At this point in the interview John rolls into his wonderful, infectious laugh and comments, "It took more than a year of this kind of experience to accept that I had been given a gift of healing."

Drawn to Massaging People with Aids

By 1983, John began to hear about this mysterious disease called AIDS. Nine people in Colorado were diagnosed with AIDS that year. John remembers that when these people finally did come into the hospital they might die within a week. John recalls:

> No one knew how to avoid catching the disease. When I asked doctors how is this disease passed, they said, "We don't know . . . We just keep washing our hands a lot."

Although he was terrified to do so, John called the Department of Health and volunteered to massage people with AIDS. "I had to go do it," John says.

> I think that's when the spiritual life began to cook really hot. That's when it began to feel like mental illness: I was terrified, I had absolutely no experience with death and dying. I had no experience with hospitals or working in medical situations. As a gay man I was terrified of getting (the disease). I thought, "Who

knows; maybe I already have it." We certainly did not have a test for it. We didn't know how long it incubated.

Not only was John afraid to work with people with AIDS, he realized that to do so jeopardized his career. "What I needed was to set up a practice with paying clients," says John. Most of the women who were suffering from abuse had been unable to pay. Most of the people with AIDS could not pay either. John knew there were plenty of paying clients at sports spas, yet no sports spa would hire John for fear of his being contaminated by working on people with AIDS.

"I had to go do it," says John of his decision to go into the hospital to work with people with AIDS.

> I think that is the real essence of a leading: you have to go do it . . . to the extent that it makes you laugh at yourself. I think if you can laugh about the amount of absurdity and the contradiction and the amount of passion that comes through, that to me is a sign of active spiritual life rather than misguided egotism.

John has an unusually strong clarity about his leading to do healing work. He says:

> One of the blessings and burdens in my leading is that I've always had a great deal of certainty. I've not had any doubt from the beginning that this is a life work.

Even with this basic clarity, there is a great deal of uncertainty about how this leading would manifest. John says,

> I did not know where it was going or what it was leading to or what it would look like. But I knew that they (my guides) had me, and I was theirs forever, and they called me to surrender.

Surrender

Surrender is one of the scariest aspects of the spiritual journey. This is the time when a person on the spiritual journey is called upon to give up ego-driven desires and to surrender to the One who calls. For a person who feels a calling, there must be a Caller, be it known as God, Jesus Christ, the Spirit of God, or one's Higher Power. A divine force is pulling and one is called to follow. This is usually a time of great fear. One is called to let go of what one knows and step into the unknown. One must let go of one trapeze bar and hope that one can catch the next one coming along.

John experienced a great deal of fear mixed with a great deal of awe. "Once I did surrender, it cooked even hotter," reports John. He recalls working on a fellow who was covered with cancer. "He was in a lot of pain and he was terrified," says John. "When I put my hands on him to begin the massage, my hands got very, very hot and all of his fear left him, his pain left him, and he went into a deep sleep." John was overwhelmed with what was happening. John remembers thinking, "This probably is not Swedish Massage. It is probably something a little different." He realized that something large was going on.

John's palms began to peal from the intense heat. This worried John because his pathology teacher at massage school had taught the students that if your palms itch and you have a rash, there is a possibility of a secondary syphilis. What a relief it was when John had it confirmed that this was not the case for him. "It was either heaven or hell and it turned out to be heaven," laughs John.

John began to focus more on doing energy work rather than massage. He was able to design a combination of the two that would take someone in terrible emotional pain or physical pain and put them completely at rest without pain or panic. The pain would not necessarily be healed forever. For a person who is in chronic pain, however, it can be a great blessing to be even temporarily calm and pain-free. John says:

> Once a person has gotten to that place of calm, then it is easier to get back there. Once you understand the concept of safe harbor, and you understand that there is a trail there, then it is easy to find the way back.

Paying the Bills

Although John was building a practice, he had trouble paying his bills. "Almost to the person my clients were too poor to pay." John washed muffin tins at a friend's bakery at night to earn some money. John pondered how to make a living.

At one point John considered setting up a school. He recalls thinking:

> I've been a school teacher. What I need to do is to open up a school so that people with AIDS will learn how to relax and how to fight their disease. They will lose their pain and therefore not die.

At that point in his life, he considered death to be the enemy. By now he has worked with dying people long enough to know death may be what needs to happen and that healing may take place on a spiritual level although the physical body dies.

A friend had a suggestion. He told John how Beethoven, at the end of his life, was supported by patrons. Maybe John's friends would help support this work of service to others. So John sent out what he called a "Beethoven Letter" to one hundred friends telling them,

> I'm working on these people with this mysterious disease. I have the support of the health department, but I do not have financial support.

Fifty people wrote back with offerings. John recalls, "Some sent money, some sent vegetables, and one person sent a typewriter." John's friends sent enough money so that he did not go hungry. He shared a house with other people and drove an "ancient" VW. "I was living on maybe $3,000 a year," he recalls. "It was very hand to mouth." What John did not realize was that asking for donations would be his way of surviving economically for many years, possibly for the rest of his life.

Spiritual Support

Spiritual surrender into a life of service cannot be done alone. One needs support and guidance. John was fortunate to find a spiritual mentor, Jean Schweitzer, one of his teachers at the massage school. John was amazed by her psychic abilities. One day when the regular pathology teacher was absent, Jean took the class. A student asked her a question about soft tissue. Jean looked at the student who was wearing big winter boots and said, "Oh, you want to know about the frostbite on the big toe of your left foot." The student responded that Jean was right on target.

In private talks with Jean, John discussed personal issues the work raised for him. John had grown up in an alcoholic and abusive home and had experienced rape by incest as a young child. While he was working with his therapist on issues from childhood as well as present issues, he also worked with Jean on the spiritual aspects of his life. John recalls how Jean once helped him to deal with a relationship that had broken up. John says, "I was crazy with anger and jealousy and rage; I was just a basket case." John recalls:

> Jean reached her arms around me, and suddenly I understood that I was to use this experience for

learning and to get ready for the person I was supposed to be with. And I was to stop all this tantrum.

John laughs, remembering that he was able to let that relationship go. "Talking with Jean saved me $2,000 in therapy bills," says John, laughing.

Jean never worked with John on how to do healing work. That was always understood to be divinely inspired. What she helped him with was getting quiet and centered. She told him he had to strengthen his capacity for stillness. He had to learn what brought him to center and what took him away from center.

Jean told John:

> You have angels who will guide you, but you are going to have to open yourself to that guidance and to their help. You have to talk with them.
>
> Get yourself some regular quiet and try not to hear yourself. Realize the immensity of the world and know you are a very small piece in it. Deflect as much as possible the noise that comes in from the world, particularly the noise you gather within your own life as you go through your life.

John was not used to thinking in such a way. It was all new to him. He says, "The disciplines we worked on for me, in particular, were stillness and quiet every day, as much as I was able." He chuckles, "And I was not able." John admits that to become quiet is still a very hard discipline for him.

Receiving Messages

As John grew in his capacity to listen inwardly, he began to receive unusual messages. They sometimes came in symbolic form. One day he was in the Salvation Army Thrift Store, shopping for his "fabulous wardrobe" when he was getting an inner message to buy a large old suitcase. This message did not come in words. It was more like an impulse to do something, like a message in meeting for worship. It had an intuitive feeling to it and an element of humor.

John recalls talking back to his guides. He responded silently. "What do you mean? Why?" The message came back, "Just do it." So he bought the suitcase. Then came the message to buy another suitcase. Before he knew it he had six large suitcases. He was living in a very small room at the time with no room for six suitcases. He remembers, "They were sitting there when I got two invitations, one to go to Friends for Lesbian and Gay Concerns mid-winter gathering and another to Oberlin College." He was writing songs about the AIDS epidemic at the time so he could lecture and give concerts. Traveling to do teaching and singing felt very good to John. Of course he did not need six suitcases to go on this trip. Why was it six suitcases? Could it be that these signs are exaggerated so that one will notice them?

When John returned home from this first speaking and singing trip, more invitations began to come to him to travel and teach. From then on his ministry included not only hands-on-healing but also teaching workshops all over the country. At this time he reports working with about 1,600 people a year, some through hands-on-healing and some through lectures and workshops. His work calls for about twenty trips a year.

Leading workshops has given him many blessings. He receives guidance as he leads them. As fifty people come into a room where he is to begin the workshop, John may recognize certain people will be his to work with even though he has never seen them before. He says, "I know the nature of their pain." He knows if they will let him, he will be able to work with them. John feels very blessed to have this kind of divine guidance. "You can't possibly receive those messages without a lot of quiet and a lot of surrender," he says.

Prayer

John's intention is to remain in touch with divine guidance as much as he can. He thinks of prayer as being in two parts, asking for help and saying "Thank you." John is not reticent to ask God for specific things to happen to him, such as saying, "Dear God in heaven, take me back to Vermont." He prays for guidance, "I would like this particular kind of guidance and I would like it sometime soon." But when working on another person, he says that it is not an option to ask that something happen. In his work, he can ask for someone to be released from something or that that person may come to a better understanding of it. "It's a short menu," he comments.

> There is a sense that you are one part of a vehicle. You can understand yourself to be either the gasoline or the rudder, but that you have only one part of the vehicle and that you are being used with the other parts.

Many times he does not know why he is to work on someone. One woman whom he was teaching in a workshop came to him for help. "We worked a long time," he says. In contrast to most of his clients she had plenty of money. She is the only client who has ever told him, "Money is no object." He reports, "Each time she felt better and better and better. But it was never clear what her issues were." John reports:

> I would be working on her and I would be saying to (my inner guides), "What the hell is going on here? We are doing all this work and you know there is no catharsis. She seems to be a little bit better each time." The message I kept getting back was, "Just keep putting in; just keep putting in. That's all you are supposed to do. And don't ask for anything in particular."

John recalls how frustrating it was:

> I wanted a clue. I could feel the spring water coming out of my hands and (I could sense) her thirst. I couldn't see where it was collecting and what it was going to be used for.

A year and a half later this woman went on a spiritual retreat. She was all alone. There she recovered the memory of her own childhood rape. John comments that he thinks she needed that time of safe touch to accumulate safety and goodness and comfort. Then on her own schedule she could go do this on her own.

John laughs at himself, saying, "They (my guides) have been very patient with me. I'm sure there are times when they are thinking, tomorrow we're going to use direct mail with him."

Avoiding Taking on a Client's Feelings or Diseases

Staying centered during a treatment session is one of John's top priorities. He says that staying centered is a way to avoid taking on other people's feelings or diseases while doing massage. "It has partly to do with posture, " he says.

> You want to be in a posture which is very open-hearted, which essentially means that your sternum, your breast bone is forward. It is almost as if you are about to sing opera. You make sure your feet are very relaxed and open and flat on the floor.

John explains:

> One of the important things when you are doing the work of helping other people with their monsters is that you have to make your own interior life very large so that your primary experience is not what you are witnessing in someone else's life. Your pri-

mary experience is your own life of the Spirit. This is what will help you go into absolutely hellish situations. This will keep you from mistaking your pain for someone else's pain. So you don't assume someone else's tension or their assumptions about the nature of life. You are not absorbing it physically or emotionally or intellectually.

John found the hardest aspect of his work was to witness pain without running to the rescue. He had to be careful not to let all the passion he had around his own issues get in the way. He had to put his own issues to the side.

As he begins a treatment, John thinks about being in meeting for worship. John likes the expression used by seventeenth-century Friends, "Never leave meeting for worship." This means staying in touch with your inner guidance.

You are holding someone's feet and you experience (the energy) going through you, and if you are open enough you can experience it almost as if it were your own feeling. But in the back of your mind you have the old hymn running. You have patience and the knowledge that this (energy from your client) is just coming up and it will wash right through you.

At the end of such a treatment both the client and John feel better.

Burnout

It has been difficult to find the right balance between work and rest, between time with clients and time alone, between traveling around the country and being home. John's practice and his teaching schedule continued to grow. Once John's gifts were known and people found relief from their pain, more and more people asked him for help. He has continued his work with women who have been sexually abused. This is still his largest practice. In addition to these women and the men dying of AIDS, a third group of people came to him for help: torture victims from Central America, from Asia, from all over the world. Again, in many cases, he was able to facilitate release from emotional and physical pain.

Sometimes the demands on John become overwhelming. At one point he spent some time in the inner city of Washington, D.C. working in a church basement with Central American refugees who had been tortured. In addition to that he was also working in six city hospitals with people dying of AIDS. That year his teaching schedule included thirty-three out-of-town trips. John's greatest challenge that year was being present to six good friends as they were dying. Not surprisingly, John went into a state of burnout.

A few good friends convinced him to take a three-months break at Pendle Hill, a Quaker Center near Philadelphia. The only way his friends could convince him to go was to suggest that he could use the time to write a book about his experiences in healing. He received grants and scholarships which paid his tuition.

Rest, Nightmares, and Recovery

In a report to his friends, John writes:

> Something that really shocked me at first was the amount of sleeping I did. During the first week I began to sleep eight to nine hours at night . . . On top of that I often caught a morning and then an afternoon nap, bringing me up to as much as fifteen hours a day of sleep. At first I thought it was wonderful. But by the second week I began to feel it was decadent. By the third week I began to wonder if I needed blood tests. Then suddenly I didn't need to sleep so much. I had more energy and a great deal more time to use it.

It was about this time that a series of nightmares came to me. It became clear that much of my tiredness, if not most of it, had to do with recovering memories of early childhood sexual assault. The work of retrieving and deeply feeling old wounds amidst my other tasks took its toll on me in many ways. Now I had the time for some clarity and taking care of the child within me.

John reports getting excellent help from a therapist on staff. He says:

This piece of my time at Pendle Hill was as important as any other and accounted for a much greater understanding of myself—both my gifts and my needs.

Since then John has learned how to pace himself so that he will not get so overtired. He now takes off six weeks between Thanksgiving and New Years, plus several week-long rests throughout the year. And he has learned to say, "no."

One of the most stabilizing aspects of John's life has been, and continues to be, his long-time relationship with Marshall Brewer. It gives John tremendous grounding for his life and work. John and Marshall met shortly after John moved to Vermont. The two were one of the first gay couples married under the care of a Friends Meeting in New England. Putney Friends Meeting took the marriage under its care in 1987.

John describes himself as "painfully shy," which can be a cross to bear for someone whose life work demands a heavy schedule of teaching at conferences and workshops. His quiet home in the country with a man he loves provides the essential balance to his dedicated service in the world.

Discernment—Learning to Say "No"

John has had to learn to say, "no." There are always a lot of demands upon his time. He can't work with everyone who feels the need for healing. But he has found out that he can work on those who are truly given to him. John has been learning to discern to whom he is supposed to say "yes" and to whom he is supposed to say "no."

> I listen to the guidance as to whether or not I am going to be able to help this person. There are times when someone comes to me when I am exhausted but the blessing to work on them is very evident, so this energy would come through me. I would feel better, and they would feel better after my working on them.

John cannot help everyone. "It is individual," he says. "The blessing I have for releasing pain in people is not a universal one. There are lots of people to whom I will be of no help whatsoever." John explained that he doesn't have a clue as to how this works.

> It has something to do with timing; it has something to do with the other person's reception; it has something to do with how that person was hurt and how they understand getting well.

Teaching Other People How To Avoid Burnout

In order to be present to people who are in great pain, John had to develop a strong ability to keep centered in the Spirit and to let go of the idea of rescuing anyone. John teaches other people how to do this kind of intense work without going into "burnout." He says:

> For a lot of people in the beginning of their helping time, a lot of their passion for giving comes from their desire for receiving. When I teach about burnout in emergency rooms, I see this all the time. A person's capacity to relax, to be calm for their own well being is almost nonexistent. But their capacity to calm down

someone who has just come in from a car wreck, whose arm is lying on a separate table, is exquisite. John points out that these are two separate capacities. In order to avoid burnout, these emergency room workers must be able to connect the two, to learn how to receive the calm for themselves as they deliver the calm for others.

In his pamphlet, *The Dance Between Hope and Fear* (p. 10), John tells how he receives the calm for himself.

> Once, when I was working with a healer and learning about my gift, I came to a time when people's pain was passing out of them, but remaining within me. It was a very hard time. I went to this healer and said, "Jean, I cannot do this work. It is much too difficult, much too difficult, because all of the sadness, all of the despair, and all of the physical pain is staying within me." And she said, "You're not saying your prayers, are you? You're not saying your prayers. Did you think you were going to do something beautiful, and it was going to be easy? Did you think you were going to do something large and it would be simple? You have to say your prayers before you do your work. And you have to say your prayers after you do your work."
>
> So here I was, massage therapist, driving around, working on people, and I thought, "Prayers, my God! I'm in rush-hour traffic, I can't be doing prayers! What am I going to do? I'm working in hospitals, I'm working in people's homes, and sometimes I go to a prison—where am I going to say my prayers?" Then I realized, as a massage therapist, that of course I have to wash my hands before and after I do my work. So I would go into the bathroom, and I would say my prayers while I washed my hands.

In this pamphlet (p. 8), John lists six sayings you can use to check in with yourself, to see where you are by which is easiest for you to say and which is the most difficult. John says, "You can listen to the people around you, the people you're working with, the people you're trying to help, and see which of these six sayings you hear them say easily, and which you never hear them express at all. These six sayings are basically all the important messages that one person can give to another:

I love you.
I'm sorry.
Thank You.
I need help.
That's not good enough.
No.

Released Friend

Ever since John first began to do his healing work he has been supported financially, spiritually, and emotionally, by an amazing number of people. Officially, he is a "released Friend," released by Putney Friends Meeting to do his work. This means his ministry is under the care of Putney Friends Meeting. People who appreciate John's work and wish to support it financially send checks to Putney Meeting for a special fund in John's name. Several members of the meeting serve on a committee which provides oversight and help as needed.

John says that the way you raise money is to go out and do something beautiful and then say, "Who will help me?" This has worked for John. He is extremely grateful for the generosity of his supporters, and for the blessings of his life.
He says:

When kids in school find some work to do that really engages them, although it is hard and they have to concentrate and focus, that is a high point for every teacher and child. When I consider that dynamic, I think of myself as an extremely blessed person be- cause the work that I have is extremely hard work, it calls for and uses all of me, and it cannot be done easily or quickly. I feel incredibly fortunate to have it and incredibly fortunate about my life.

John does not expect his leading to come to an end. John admits that his work might shift.

Maybe the pace will change. Maybe the group I am going to be working with is going to change. But the essence of what I am going to do is . . . they (my guides) have me and they are going to use me.

Looking back over his faith journey, John comments, "When I took the leap, I had the faith I would find a net; instead I learned to fly."

XI. CREATIVITY AND HEALING

Arla Patch

Arla Patch

The Journey

*One day you finally knew
what you had to do, and began,
though the voices around you
kept shouting
their bad advice—
though the whole house
began to tremble
and you felt the old tug
at your ankles.
"Mend my life!"
each voice cried.
But you didn't stop.
you knew what you had to do,
though the wind pried
with its stiff fingers
at the very foundations,
though their melancholy
was terrible.*

*It was already late
enough, and the wild night,
and the road full of fallen
branches and stones.
But little by little,
as you left their voices behind,
the stars began to burn
through the sheets of clouds,
and there was a new voice
which you slowly
recognized as your own,
that kept you company
as you strode deeper and deeper
into the world,
determined to do
the only thing you could do—
determined to save
the only life you could save.*

—Mary Oliver

D riving two hours north from Portland, Maine, you skirt the edge of the White Mountains. The road dips into valleys and then rises to ridges from which you can view the grey blue hills. As the pavement gives way to gravel, the road climbs up to Arla Patch's hilltop home. As I drive up the steep slope, I wonder what the road is like in winter.

A friendly golden retriever bounds over to greet me. Arla and her eighteen-year-old son, Per, are just behind. Arla leads me into the three-story wooden house which perches on the side of a mountain. Arla designed the home, acted as contractor, and worked alongside the carpenters hammering in the nails. She is particularly proud of designing the windowseat, deep enough and comfortable enough to use as a double bed . Three sides of the bed are windows with a panoramic view over the wooded valley and the Presidential Range.

Paintings and plaster masks decorate the walls. Arla leads me up to the third level where she has her studio. Projects made by children in her art classes hang from a wire. Arla is an experienced teacher; she has a master's degree in fine arts and has been teaching art to adults and children for twenty-six years.

Taking advantage of the beautiful afternoon, we climb the mountain behind the house, following a trail that leads through a woods of spruce, pine, birch, oak and maple trees. When we finally get to the rocky outcropping which is Arla's special place, we sit silently in worship together. This is Arla's daily spiritual practice, climbing to this rock for her prayers, even in the winter by snowshoe. We watch the light become golden and the shadows lengthen, then head down for dinner.

Arla and her husband have a blended family including their two sons, one from each of their first marriages. The sons were ages four and six when this second marriage began a dozen years ago. Now they are in their late teens, one in college and one a senior in high school. Arla puts a lot of nurturing energy into enjoying her children in a way she never was nurtured herself.

Through art, Arla has found a way to heal herself from the scars of her childhood and to use the sensitivity this experience gave her for the service of others. Now in her late forties, she facilitates workshops helping other people to turn their wounds into positive channels for the Spirit through creating masks and breastplates, expressing themselves with passion through art.

M.C. Richards, in her book Centering *(pp. 12-13), writes* about the passion of creativity:

But of course we have to be passionate. That is to say, when we are, we must be able to be. We must be able to let the intensity—the Dionysian rapture and disorder and the celebration of chaos, of potentiality, the experience of surrender—we must be able to let it live in our bodies, in our hands, through our hands into the materials we work with. I sense this: that we must be steady enough in ourselves, to be open and to let the winds of life blow through us, to be our breath, our inspiration; to breathe with them, mobile and soft in the limberness of our bodies, in our agility, our ability, as it were, to dance, and yet to stand upright, to be intact, to be persons. We come to know ourselves, and others, through the images we create in such moods. These images are disclosures of ourselves to ourselves. They are life-revelations. If we can stay "on center" and look with clear-seeing eyes and compassionate hearts at what we have done, we may advance in self-knowledge and in knowledge of our materials and of the world in its larger concerns.

There is a wonderful legend in Jewish Hasidism that in the begining when God poured out his grace, man was not able to stand firm before the fullness and the vessels broke and sparks fell out of them into all things. And shells formed around them. By our *hallowing, we may help to free these sparks. They lie everywhere, in our tools, in our food, in our clothes . . . a kind of radiance, an emanation, a freedom, something that fills our hearts with joy and gratitude no matter how it may strike our judgment! There is something within man that seeks this joy. That knows this joy. Joy is different from happiness. I am not talking about happiness. I am talking about joy. How, when the mind stops its circling, we say Yes, Yes to what we behold.*

Arla loves to see participants free these sparks of joy. Her students teach her lessons and give her clues. Arla was nudged by a participant in a mask-making workshop to help her make a "breastplate." Since then, Arla has led many breastplate workshops for women. Participants make plaster casts of their torsos, including their breasts and sometimes stomach and shoulders, and then decorate them in a way that gives expression to their deepest feelings about themselves.

Facilitating these workshops has been a spiritually deepening experience for Arla. Her most recent work has been to facilitate breastplate workshops for breast cancer survivors, many of whom have lost one or both breasts to mastectomy.

Childhood

"My childhood was a time of devastating physical, emotional and sexual abuse at the hands of both my parents," says Arla. Her parents were divorced when Arla was ten years old.

There were times when I was praised, such as for being a good student, but that was what made the abuse so confusing and crazy making. What I did feel was that I was not seen for who I really was or valued just because I existed. Any value reflected was

197

so conditional, and then coupled with times of abuse, it made me feel the few times of positive regard were lies. I began to feel there was no speck of me that was good. That makes it hard to believe it when any-one gives a compliment.

She explains:

The effect of early and prolonged abuse is that it erodes your sense of yourself at the very core. It leaves you with a feeling of not being seen, not de-serving much, and the feeling that there is some-thing essentially wrong with you from your center on out. That makes it hard to believe it when anyone gives a compliment.

Arla's family moved a great deal, from country to coun-try, because her father was in the military. The family lived for a while in Naples, Italy. Arla graduated from high school in Bangkok, Thailand. She studied art during college in Rome.

Although Arla speaks of a childhood devoid of the kind of parenting she needed, she also speaks of being given gifts by the Spirit. She retains a strong memory of a spiri-tual awakening at age ten. Her parents had just separated. Arla's mother, with all her children, moved to a farm house. Arla recalls:

I ran out in the field. It had been freshly plowed, and it was very soft. I was trying to run across the field and go down to the edge where there were these big trees I liked to climb, right beside the creek. As I ran through the field I realized I was sinking into the mud. My memory is that I was sunk almost up to my knees. I had one of those still moments of realizing that I was utterly connected to everything and that I was planted in the earth. I could feel the layers of the atmosphere; it felt like my head was in the sky.

Arla says that experience told her there was "something there that was bigger and that I was a part of and that I was also being cared for within that." She held that experience in her heart, even making a sculpture of it when she was in college; it now sits in her hallway.

That experience became a touchstone for Arla. She knows that in spite of all she went through, she has been under divine care for her entire life. The more she awakens to Spirit, the more she understands that the care and guidance have always been there. Arla says, "To me, the whole journey is one of awakening. From birth to death is a series of awakenings. People are on different stages of awakening, from fast asleep to fully enlightened, like Buddha and Jesus." This way of looking at life helps Arla to forgive her own parents.

When Arla was about twelve years old, living in Doylestown, Pennsylvania, not long after she had that mystical experience, she became friends with a young Quaker. This girl invited Arla to her house. Arla loved the peace and quiet of this Quaker home. This family took Arla to a Friends meeting for worship with them. This was a turning point in her life. She continued to attend meeting but it took her awhile before she developed enough trust and feeling of worth to join. In her late twenties, after sixteen years of attending meeting, she became a member of the Religious Society of Friends. Her Quaker faith continues to be a fundamental aspect of her life and of the way she sees herself today.

Young Adult

As a young woman Arla studied art education and taught in schools first in Pennsylvania and then in Maine. She married and had a son.

She is a high achiever. She has always been successful in her outer life, but she has had a lot of inner healing to do. After she moved to Maine in 1986, she began to do healing from childhood destructive influences. She and her husband divorced, sharing custody of their son, Per. Per has lived with Arla half the time and with his father half the time. Later, Arla met and married her present husband.

Lorenzo

About six years ago something happened that changed Arla's life. A little red-headed boy named Lorenzo was going to take her summer program, an art class. The boy's mother is an artist and an art teacher, and Arla had met Lorenzo a few times when he was too young to take the program. He would come to the program's art show with his mother. Arla says,

> I was real excited that he was signed up and was going to take the class. Just before the summer started his mother called and said Lorenzo had gotten Leukemia and he would be going to Boston and getting treatments. She wanted to take the money for him and make it a special scholarship for some other child.

"I was so touched by that and so moved." says Arla. "I couldn't stand the idea that maybe this little boy was not going to make it. I threw in the towel and said, 'Okay, I'm praying.'" Arla explains that she had not been able to pray openly before.

> I went to meeting for worship, and I certainly was praying in a form that I did not acknowledge as prayer. But I never really just got down, right down there, and opened right up and tried to open the line of communication.

Arla has been taking hikes up her mountain for a long time as a way to get centered, to get peace, to think about her life and to pray. She calls it "Meeting in motion." The uphill is always a walk. Sometimes she runs down. Once she heard about Lorenzo, when she got to the highest point of the hike she opened up and asked God to hold Lorenzo in the Light, to please allow this child to have the life that he was meant to have, whatever that is. She says, "As a result of praying for Lorenzo I began to develop a practice of prayer."

Hiking up the mountain every other day has become a spiritual practice. Six years later she is happy to report Lorenzo is a fifth grader in her art program. He is still in her prayer and there are eight or nine other people as well.

This is a prayer Arla says on a regular basis:

> Creator, sustainer, and my true parent, please may I be open to your love and your guidance. Please may I draw to me all the appropriate people, places, things, realizations, understandings, resources and opportunities that I may do the work that I am meant to do.

Sometimes she simply says a phrase she learned from working with rune stones, "I will to will Thy will."

Mask Making

Not long after that Arla participated in a mask-making workshop. The participants were paired up. She had never done this and the person doing it with her had never done it either. They took turns putting the strips of gauze impregnated with plaster on each other's faces. Arla's partner put the gauze strips straight down over Arla's mouth so that when they pulled off the mask, there was no mouth. There were no lips. Her partner was upset and very apologetic. Arla's response was, "Hey, don't worry about it; I'm sure there's a reason for this."

Indeed there was. This mask became another turning point for Arla. She took the mask home, gazed at it, held it in her hands, took it in, and continued to work on it. She rubbed charcoal around the inside of the eyes and the incredible sadness of the mask came forward. At that point Arla realized the mask was about the fact that when she was abused as a child she did not have a voice. She never knew she could say, "No," or "Leave me alone." Not long before this Arla had watched a teacher telling her children they could say, "Leave me alone," or "Don't touch me," and Arla had burst into tears, wishing someone had given her that permission when she was a child.

Working on the mask, Arla made a circle where the mouth would have been and then wider and wider circles fading to nothing. She used a glue gun to stick stones on to look like tears. The stones did not look right so she took them off, but the globs of dried glue became tears. On top she added feathers. As she looked at it, the feathers seemed to be a connection with "my crown." When she was done she looked at the mask and thought, "The mask has taught me. The mask has power. The mask can help me to heal."

Healing has been central for Arla for many years now. Like many women who suffered sexual abuse in childhood, Arla continues to work through feelings of not being worthy. She explains, "Sexual abuse makes you feel like you are tainted goods . . . you are bad. There is something bad at the core of you instead of being something good at the core of you." It takes a long time to change this self-image.

Another difficulty was the fact that in church God was referred to as "the Father." Arla comments, "Now if your father is your main perpetrator, that really blocked the relationship with God. It just didn't work."

When Arla moved to Maine she joined several women's groups and became involved in women's spirituality. This spiritual awakening was connected to her healing process as a whole. All of this began to be reflected in Arla's own work. She began to lead mask-making workshops and sometimes she made a mask herself. One time she was leading a guided meditation in a mask-making workshop when she had a vision come to her. She relates:

What happened was this feeling of gratefulness came to me. I saw a face and felt the sound, "aaaaahhh"—a heart sound. I saw the face, her mouth was slightly open. Her eyes were closed. On top of her head was this shape like a spray of flowers. I saw that shape as godhead, connecting to the divine through my crown center.

Arla created a mask to represent that vision. She says:

The mask turned out exactly like the image. It was very validating; it showed me a lot of healing had happened. I was slowly accepting the God in me. That is one of the hardest things for a survivor of childhood abuse.

The more Arla awakens to Spirit, the more she finds herself guided in what she does. She remarks:

The leading is there. It is up to me to pay attention and recognize it as a leading. It is not me having the leading or creating the leading. It is me getting out of the way so I can recognize the leading. I am co-creating. I have to be awake enough to see what Spirit is doing and appreciate and acknowledge it.

"I Want To Do My Breasts!"

Often a person is driven to prayer by a challenge of some sort. Arla was driven to prayer by the prospect of teaching a mask-making workshop for the staff at Omega Institute, an institute for Holistic Studies in New York state which offers summer workshops. Arla had participated in a workshop and applied to teach an art program there. Omega invited her to teach mask-making to the staff the following summer. "I was scared to death," she recalls.

I had many weird dreams before I went. I knew the only way I could get through it was to pray every

> chance I could. So when I got to my little room I just
> prayed. And before meals I prayed. I got into a state
> and it just flowed.

Arla remembers there was much excitement and energy
in her workshop that week. Then the big challenge came.

> I had a wonderful woman who was fifty-five. After
> she made her mask, I shared with her what I saw in
> it. She had such beautiful bone structure that the
> mask had classic beauty, strength, and female power.
> We both acknowledged that. When she saw that, she
> grabbed both her hands to her breasts and said, "I
> want to do my breasts." I said, "What a great idea!
> Why not?"

Arla points out this was a moment of being nudged by
the Spirit. "This woman was sent by God . . . I needed to
recognize that." The minute the woman said it, Arla realized
the potential:

> The breast area is the heart center for all of us; for
> women it is a place of sexuality, a place of the lead-
> ing cancer deaths, a place where we've nurtured our
> children. It is a place of incredible judgment because
> one's breasts are never right, never good enough.

At the same time Arla realized the hazards of working in
this area, the fact that this would bring up fear and many
other emotions. "I knew the only way to do this was to make
the workshop as sacred as possible and as safe as possible."
Arla sees the work she does as creating that kind of safe and
sacred space. When that is in place, Arla feels what she calls
"a synergy" between the person, Spirit, and the materials.

Arla asked her supervisor whether she could schedule such
a workshop later in the summer for a group of staff women.
The supervisor scheduled it. When Arla returned to Omega
a month later she found the workshop was fully enrolled
and had a long waiting list. Arla added another section

of her workshop so she could take in the women on the waiting list.

One of the ways Arla knows she is on the right track is by affirmations from what she calls "the universe." For instance, the gauze she needed for a workshop like this is very expensive. The nurse at Omega came up with a whole box of gauze for her to use.

An even greater affirmation is when a person is helped or healed in some way by the art work they do. At her first breastplate workshop, one of the participants, Jane (not her real name) confided to Arla that she was in an unhealthy relationship. Jane was not being treated with dignity. She talked about her feelings and about the fact that she did not know how to get out of the relationship. Arla asked if she wanted to express her frustration and anger. When Jane began to decorate her breastplate, she surprised Arla with the courage and forcefulness she showed. She drove to town and purchased a can of bronze spray paint and sprayed her breastplate with it. She created a mask with a headdress that made Arla think it looked like it belonged to a queen.

Arla was thrilled.

> I was in complete elation because it was so powerful. She didn't go for angry. She went for powerful. Her breastplate and mask were saying, "This is my presence. I'm here."

Arla remembers laughing and hugging Jane and telling her, "This is claiming your space."

After all the breastplates were decorated, the group took time to look at all of them and listen to what people had to say. Then Arla offered a chance to go one step further. She explained that one aspect of art is making the piece. Another aspect of art is choosing to share it, or not to share it, with others. Arla had permission to hang any of the masks and breastplates that participants chose to exhibit in the staff dining room.

Jane said she was terrified to share hers in this co-educational community because she had always been embarrassed about her breasts being pendulous and she did not see herself as an artist. She had never done much with art before. Arla recalls:

> The day I was going to hang all the work, Jane showed up and said she had thought about it and journaled about it and she had decided to exhibit her mask and breastplate. So we both carried them over into the dining room and hung them up. We hung the mask above the breastplate so it made a complete sculpture. Immediately men and women came over. They seemed to be in awe of it and Jane felt that. She burst into tears and I held her. We both cried because it was such a huge step for her. It was art, and it was her.

A year later this woman told Arla that doing the breastplate and mask had profoundly shifted something for her.

Arla loves to work with women who have never done art. Many times she is profoundly moved by their work and their comments on their work. Arla choked up as she told me about one woman who was sanding her breastplate and said, "O my God, I made a work of art. And it came from my body . . . so I must be a work of art."

Every time a participant has a healing experience in her workshop, Arla is healed a little more herself. She feels these workshops are Spirit led. She says:

> I don't think we even begin to understand the forces that are at work and the way this whole business works, we are just groping our way. We simply have to open to it and allow it.

Affirmation

After Arla returned home she was invited to do breastplate workshops in Maine.

Again the cost of the impregnated gauze was an obstacle. She called Johnson and Johnson. The man with whom she talked told her he needed to know she was in business. So she sent him letters and faxes, explaining that she was doing workshops for healing through art. She was hoping to get a good price on buying a lot of gauze all at once. All summer she tried to contact this man without success.

One day she had a phone call from this man. He said, "I've sent you a case; it is coming special delivery. You will get it in two days. And don't worry about it." Arla asked him what he meant by "Don't worry about it." She queried, "Do you mean it is like a gift from the universe?"

He laughed and said, "Yea, a gift from the universe." She found out later that at the end of the year, sometimes for public relations a person may give such a gift. Whatever his motive, Arla took this as a sign from the Spirit that she was on the right track.

> It was such an enormous boost and it was much more than the financial aspect, it was the unbelievable af-firmation that I should be doing the work. Because here was someone saying, "Here is the material; do the work."

Inner Work

In order to do this work in the world, Arla needs to do her own inner work. These mask-making and breastplate work-shops have stretched Arla in new and challenging ways. She says to lead a person through a deep healing experience is like being a midwife to a woman having a baby. Arla works with a therapist and a body worker. She likes to take trou-bling issues into solitude and work with them using artistic media. At this time she gives thanks for all she has received. Once a year she takes a solo retreat. She rents a little cabin by a lake and stays for three days. This time alone allows her to deal with deep issues that have been coming up in her life as well as to reconnect with herself and Spirit and to absorb the blessings that have come.

Arla sees her own inner work as vital to being a good facilitator. Each time she can work through her fears, she is learning how to hold another person while that person works through feelings of fear as he or she creates art.

Spiritual community is another aspect of staying centered. In order to lead transformative workshops, Arla relies on her spiritual home. She helped form a new meeting in Maine and served as the first clerk. A clearness committee from the meeting helped her affirm doing the breastplate workshops. A "clearness committee" in the Quaker tradition is a group of Friends who sit with you in prayer to help you become centered and help you become clear about what should be your next steps as you are nudged by God.

Money Issues

Arla explains it is challenging for her to be in business for herself and have to set fees. "It forces me to acknowledge what I am worth. I have to walk around in my skin as being worth it and being able to make a living." It was different when she worked in public school and received a regular pay check every other week.

Money is for Arla, as it is for most of us, an emotional issue. Arla connects it to her history as an abuse survivor.

> I still hold this belief that unless I am really poor and really struggling that I am not worthy. I am needing to understand abundance and understand flow and giving.

It has been so important for Arla that she used her grant money to offer scholarships for her workshops. When she went to introduce her workshop proposal to the first breast cancer group, she was very happy that she could offer scholarships. She could tell them that anyone, regardless of how much they could pay, would be welcome to participate.

A New Challenge

Arla realized that making breastplates was a healing experience for many of the participants. She decided to offer this workshop, which she calls "To Cherish Our Bodies: A Woman's Breastplate" to women who had experienced breast cancer. Arla's own mother had a mastectomy so Arla had some understanding of what this was like. Arla contacted a women's health center and was told about a support group for women who have, or who did have, breast cancer. The leaders told her that she could come talk to the group about the possibility of participating in a breastplate workshop.

Even meeting with the group brought up inner work for Arla because of her own mother's breast cancer. Arla's mother's grandmother died of cancer. She has been told that according to certain medical profiles, she might be considered high risk for getting cancer herself. She tries to look beyond statistics like that, realizing that she is taking many positive steps towards her own emotional and physical healing, steps which would make her less susceptible to cancer.

Arla finds herself drawn to work with these women. Part of what draws her is her mother's experiences. Arla says, "I am trying to forgive my mother and heal all that. I know there is a huge piece in there for me."

Six of the women decided to do the workshop with Arla. All of them have had mastectomies. Two had double mastectomies. Several of them had reconstructive surgery.

Leading the workshop was a challenge for Arla. She says:

> I was afraid that I would not be sensitive. I wanted to be very respectful of these women. For that reason I found myself screening everything I was going to say before I said it.

The workshop went very well, and Arla was happy to hear later that the women appreciated her sensitivity.

Arla is often tired after leading a weekend workshop. But this time she was particularly drained. This was the first time she had ever seen reconstructive surgery on breasts . . . the scars instead of nipples. It was the first time she had heard such stories. One woman had a back muscle cut and made into a breast. The areola was tattooed in and skin was gathered and sewed on to look like a nipple. Arla comments, "It was sobering."

Arla was exhausted after the workshop. She says:

> I had empathized so fully with these women and listened so deeply as they talked about their experiences, I took it (the feelings of these women) on.

When this happens, Arla goes to her mountain. She climbs the path up to her favorite rock. After this workshop, which was in the winter time, she lay down on the snow and cried. She says, "I let it all go."

Arla was particularly moved when the breast cancer survivors who participated in her workshop decided to exhibit their breastplates in a gallery to raise money for breast cancer research. They found a woman who owned a gallery on a main street in Portland that was willing to do a show during October, breast cancer support month. Benefits from this show would go for breast cancer research. Although the breastplates were anonymous, all six women were there at the opening and spoke with the people who came. Next to each breastplate was a written message, a few words from the artist. These writings were a powerful addition to the exhibit.

One of the torsos was gold with flecks of red, reminiscent of blood, dripping from the suture lines. Next to it were the words: "Tell me what's wrong but make it quick."

A pink and gold, one-breaster body had a door behind the mastectomy scar. Behind that door was a hidden world of sea shells, seeds, flowers, and a pearl deeply embedded in the background. The words beside it were:

My right breast has been removed. Beneath, a new door opens. Refreshing views. I'm thinking about a second career and dancing lessons.

The artist wrote this comment:

(Coming to the breastplate workshop) I was feeling very fragile. I wanted to come to terms with what my body looked like. I wanted to feel sexy, to celebrate what I still had. I wanted to remember that dance and the ocean were still intertwined in my spirit.

Another one wrote:

I sacrificed my right breast for my life. Now I struggle with the reality that my loss brings no guarantees. I choose life. I am whole.

One woman wrote:

I conquered so many obstacles only to be faced by more. The physical treatments are done, but the emotional part is ongoing. The light is shining, and I am growing, and discovering the gifts I have been given.

Another wrote this statement:

I exist high on the timberline. It is a place of extremes. You see, the vision from here actually speaks. It sings with an intense energy emitting pure true emotion derived from an ancient chord that vibrates from the depth of my soul . . . I am like the rugged krummholz tree, purposefully and deliberately reaching deep within the earth to find strength, nourishment, meaningfulness, and answers. Enduring a bending with the prevailing winds and rough weather, I am steadfast in the quest for the essence. My spirit flows with the rhythm of life.

Arla spoke at the opening. Next to her stood the six women. "That was one of the happiest days of my life," says Arla.

> It was so deep, so important. I had a chance to speak for these women. It was not focused on me. I got to point out how important is the connection between art and healing. I was trusting my intuition and trusting that I can say what it is that I am feeling.
>
> This was the first chance for me to speak in public about this healing work I've been doing. It was another really big step in the healing I've been doing in finding my own voice.

The Arla that spoke at that opening was a far cry from the Arla who could not speak, the Arla without a mouth. It meant a lot to Arla when a woman Arla considers to be one of her mentors came up to her after the talk and said, "You spoke with such inner authority."

What Next?

A woman from North Carolina who saw the exhibit in Portland, Maine, invited Arla to come to North Carolina to lead a breastplate workshop sponsored by Allamance Regional Hospital. Using art for healing is part of this hospital's mission statement. Arla searched for a Friends meeting house in which to hold the workshop. She has used meetinghouses before and finds them to be peaceful settings for her work. She says, "People can feel the sacredness of the space where there has been a lot of worship." Cane Creek Meeting, 250-years-old and once part of the Underground Railroad, agreed to hold the event. Meeting members viewed the event as a form of outreach because most of the participants were non-Quaker. Arla found the meeting to be very supportive.

One aspect of the workshop that Arla, a northerner, never anticipated was the interracial relations. While all the participants were breast cancer survivors, some were Afro-

American and others were white. The black women were terrified to go outside at night, even to a car in the parking area. They insisted on leaving well before dark to get home in daylight, so Arla shortened the workshop on the final day to accommodate them. There was also a class difference. One woman worked in the local sock factory and did not own a car. Another was the vice-president of the Breast Cancer Coalition of North Carolina. Arla was amazed at how the focus on creating their own breastplates pulled them together as a tight community in spite of their differences in race and class. "They called themselves 'Sisters of the Breastplate,'" says Arla.

A few months later, Arla flew back for the opening of the show put on by these participants. One of the elders of the meeting, a cancer survivor herself, invited Arla to stay in her home. Members of the meeting brought fruit and filled the meetinghouse with flowers. At the end of the weekend Arla attended Cane Creek meeting for worship to show her appreciation.

A year later, as a result of a talk she gave to doctors and nurses at that hospital, Arla was invited back to lead a breastplate and mask-making workshop for the oncology nurses at that hospital. Arla explains that these nurses find their energy depleted after working with cancer patients day after day and the workshop may help them restore their energy. Another workshop for the same hospital is planned for this year.

As Arla continues to develop her skills and expertise, she is being asked to give talks. Guilford College, in North Carolina, not far from Allamance Regional Hospital, has invited her to be on a panel for Quakers and the Arts. She has begun to write a book about her experiences.

The intensity of this work has taken a lot of energy. Arla realizes she is in danger of reaching a point of burnout. It is hard for her to find the right balance of work and rest. The image of a bear appeared in one of her dreams and she realizes she needs to become more like a bear and take time for hibernation, for some alone time.

Privileged

Arla feels privileged to be able to help people experience their creativity. She says:

> Creativity is closely connected with spirituality. As a culture we don't understand the significance of creativity. The divine manifests in creativity. We are here through creativity . . . our birth is a creative act. We create by giving birth. Most people don't get a chance to hang out in their creative selves. When I create the space, time, facility, material, and opportunity for people to experience their creativity, I am helping them to connect with their spirituality.

Reflecting upon her work, Arla comments:

> This work is integrating my spiritual path, my aspect as an artist, and my interest in healing, putting them all together. It is a privilege to be a tiny cog in the wheel of helping the planet to heal.

XII. SINGING

Jacqueline Coren

Jacqueline Coren

My life flows on in endless song;
above earth's lamentation,
I hear the sweet, though far-off hymn
that hails a new creation.
Through all the tumult and the strife,
I hear that music ringing;
It sounds an echo in my soul,
how can I keep from singing?

Music: American Gospel Hymn
Words: Anonymous

*T*hirty men and women are gathering for a rehearsal. The chorus director, Jackie Coren, appears in the doorway. This slim, dark-haired, energetic woman greets her chorus warmly and hands out the evening's sheet music. Jackie jokes with the chorus as they begin the warm-up exercises. There is a spirit of fun in the room. She fills the room with lively and light-hearted energy.

At the present time, Jackie is employed on the faculty of George School, a Quaker boarding and day school near Philadelphia where she leads several different choruses, including a community chorus. Once a week she leads a chorus at Pendle Hill. Jackie is fifty-two years old and lives with her partner in a house in Philadelphia.

Jackie's calling is to encourage people to sing together. She particularly loves to work with "new singers," people who have not had much experience singing in a group. Throughout her life, Jackie has continually sought out and encouraged people to try singing. She is thrilled when one of them is able to overcome his or her mental blocks and joins in a chorus.

Jackie Coren did not have to search for her call. Her call pursued her in camp, college, graduate school, and wherever she went. My understanding of the term "call," or "calling," is that it refers to a deeply-held and long-term ministry. Leadings, in contrast, are the more time-specific opportunities along the way that guide one to a calling that can be one's life work inwardly and outwardly. Jackie's story describes her response to individual leadings that over time ground her in a life-long call to lead groups in song.

Childhood

Jackie sensed a calling very early in life. She remarks:

> I don't think when I came into this world I said "I want to be a musician." It just came over me. This is some-

thing that I find myself doing. It is hard to describe the feeling I get, but it's then that I feel my life is guided. It just does grab me. And I'm grateful.

Raised as a Conservative Jew, Jackie says:

The music was especially meaningful to me, and I entered into the mystery of that faith most deeply through the sung liturgy. I was in my element when I sang the Torah portion for my Bat Mitzvah. At that time the thought of women entering the rabbinate or cantorate was unheard of, and so I didn't recognize until later in life that that had been of interest to me as a child.

When Jackie was about twelve years old, her father, an insurance broker, gave her a banjo ukelele a client had discarded. She recalls:

On the way to summer vacation that summer I sat in the back seat of the car with this book, How to Play the Banjo Ukulele. You tune it to, (singing) "My dog has fleas." While we drove to the mountains I learned "Camptown Races" and "Oh Suzannah," picking them out by myself and being completely absorbed in that.

The next natural step was to get everyone to sing. Jackie urged her parents, "Let's all sing 'Camptown Races.'" She says, "I learned to play that little thing." Although Jackie switched to playing a five-string banjo during high school, she has always kept that banjo ukulele.

Summer Camp and College

When Jackie was a counselor at a summer camp for inner city kids, she started a small chorus of counselors. She says:

We had chapel every Sunday morning, and I got some of our counselors together to practice "Dona Nobis Pacem." I remember working on the subtleties of it.

The counselors liked it, and I liked it, too. I actually did this before I took a class in conducting. I think I had an instinct for it.

Her college life, in the 1960s, was filled with music. She attended the University of California at Berkeley. Jackie remembers:

It seems strange now, but we used to sit around in our dorm rooms in Berkeley singing freedom songs, protest songs, and folk songs. And I'd have my banjo and we'd just sing. We loved to do that. Everybody was doing that.

Music became a stabilizing force in Jackie's college life.

Just at the point when I was about to be swallowed alive by the immensity of the school and the upheaval it was experiencing, I fell "accidentally" into the music program; a college counselor suggested I take a music course. Although the language of Grace was not given to me until years later, I felt in my heart that I had come home.

Jackie eventually majored in music with an emphasis on choral directing. She says:

I was not as skilled or experienced as many of my peers, but I know now that I was compelled and was given the energy and "chutzpah" to explore the art intuitively and effectively. I loved it. I really did.

Initially, she felt inadequate to some of the course work in the music department because she had come to this study later than many of the students and she questioned her own ability. "I loved singing, but I didn't have a particularly good voice," she says. She was enrolled in a group voice class and her teacher helped her. Whenever a student expressed nervousness about singing in front of the group, the teacher announced in her strong Welsh accent, "False pride!" Jackie recalls, "She made us want to get up and sing in front of each other." Jackie comments that this experience, singing in front of a group, gave her confidence in speaking up in other classes as well:

> In another class, one set of exercises involved coordinating our piano and singing skills. I was pretty slow at this, but I worked hard, determined to improve. Again, we had to perform in front of the group, and I remember one day bringing in an exercise I had worked very hard on. When it was my turn, I went to the piano and performed the exercise flawlessly! A major triumph for me. The teacher then turned to the class and said, "Well, that was very good; now, who'd like to try it? If Jackie can do it, anyone can!" This may seem like a devastating remark, but it was actually very funny. We were a pretty tight group, the music students, and there was a supportive atmosphere in this class. So I didn't take it as a put-down at all. I think he was actually proud of me. He was right, of course. If I could do it, anyone in that class could!

Jackie says that this is part of what fuels her excitement for teaching. She knows from her own experience what it's like to doubt her abilities, to feel inadequate and behind. So, if after working at a task she can achieve some success, she knows that with determination, encouragement, and solid instruction, others can also.

Supported by Community

Jackie moved to Philadelphia from California in 1969. She says, "I never rejected my Judaism. It had simply moved to a back burner during college days." In Philadelphia Jackie was introduced to various forms of meditation and mystical thought through Yoga and metaphysics. She remembers this time of her life as being one of intense searching. She encountered Quakerism for the first time. She says:

> I found it very compatible with my spirituality. I was especially moved by the ethos of the "Inward Teacher." I have always been buffeted about by external demands and expectations. I was unaware of the power of inner movement and discernment.

In the mid 1970s, at a time of personal transition, Jackie joined a spiritual community. She became a student at Pendle Hill and, following her student year, stayed there for six years, three on the cooking staff and three on the teaching staff developing a music curriculum. Such communities are strong when individuals come forward to recognize and nurture the gifts of its members. There have been many such individuals for Jackie at Pendle Hill:

> There were those who listened and reflected as I struggled to discern the right direction; those who asked me to take on a new task, which helped me gain confidence; those who have been able to name my gifts clearly and directly and help me own them. I owe a lot to many people who have been with me in many ways over the years.

Jackie proposed and developed a music curriculum at Pendle Hill. She organized a small chorus (the forerunner of the present chorus) and developed courses in music listening and music in religious community. This curriculum was an innovation both for Pendle Hill at the time and for Jackie:

> I was surprised at how passionately I felt about it and about its place in the curriculum and community. I began to see parallels between corporate worship and group singing. Both encompass the union of a certain self-oriented focus and the corporate listening experience, the clear definition of self and the merging with the larger body. Ever-expanding circles of listening.

Seminary

As Jackie grew stronger in her Quaker spirituality and in her musical leadership within community, she longed for more concentrated religious education. She decided to take a Masters of Divinity degree at the Earlham School of Religion (ESR), connected with the Quaker institution, Earlham College.

> I had no clear goal in mind for my seminary training. As a "Jewish Unprogrammed Friend," pulpit ministry was not a strong draw. I only knew that I was pulled strongly towards the seminary and the program it offered. What awaited me there I could not have dreamed of or designed for myself.

When she was accepted, however, she was confronted within herself with a dilemma she hadn't expected.

> I had, for some years, comfortably moved into and around the Quaker world with little concern for discrepancies with my Jewish heritage.

Jackie remembers at that time being faced with two dilemmas. One regarded her call as a musician. She wondered if she was choosing between music and religious studies. In fact, her musical calling followed her to ESR as it had followed her everywhere else. She could not get away from it. There was a group of women at ESR who had formed a singing group, whose director was graduating. Jackie assumed leadership of the group, and over the course of the following six years she encouraged students, faculty, alumni from both ESR and the College. It grew eventually into a mixed chorus of approximately thirty singers.

> Anyone, experienced and inexperienced alike, was encouraged to sing. The union of music and the religious community once again became a strong and growing focus for me. We presented our music in worship, workshops, and social gatherings at the seminary, the College, and within the wider Indiana Quaker

community. I had, in a sense, moved into the cantorate that was closed to me within the Jewish world—but what irony to find it among Quakers!

After graduating from ESR, Jackie taught as an assistant in the choral program at Earlham College while working as a Campus Ministry Associate. It was a wonderful joining of the two trajectories of her call.

The second dilemma was more troubling and less clearly defined.

> This took me completely by surprise. Now that I was taking a decided step to move more deeply into the world of Quakerism, I wondered if I were forsaking my Judaism once and for all. Curiously, I wasn't even bothered by this thought when I joined a Quaker Meeting a short while before. But somehow going off to seminary really raised the issue in a powerful way. Answers to serious questions often come to me in humorous ways. I wrestled deeply with it, and finally I heard, "As long as you know what to put on a pastrami sandwich, you'll still be Jewish." I'm sure it's Biblical.) I understood that voice to mean that my Jewish connection was secure, that it was deeply who I am, even if I travel for a while outside the community. I was a seeker, and my searching so far had brought me to a strong and healthy community of worship, and as long as I was sincerely seeking, I would be in the right place. Until news of white bread and mayonnaise reached G--D's ear, I supposed that I would be OK.

While at ESR, this revelation opened more and more for Jackie. Courses in Hebrew Bible and Judaism directly offered opportunities to study Jewish thought; and courses in theology and religious history helped her more subtly in clarifying her own beliefs and ways of understanding. The school, recognizing the issues for Jackie, was very supportive.

They allowed me, for example to take a course in Judaism to satisfy my Church History requirement. Also, one of the final requirements to graduate is a course called Comprehensive Seminar. Each student is given a hypothetical situation, tailored to that student's particular issues or work, and we were given one week to formulate a response and make a big presentation. I was quite certain that my question would be something on music and religious life. Instead, I was to give a presentation on Jewish-Christian dialogue from a Quaker perspective to a synagogue women's group. I had to turn myself inside out and backwards for that one, and it was an amazing experience of self discovery.

After graduation, in her work at the College, Jackie once again faced the dilemma of her Quaker-Jewish leanings in a disturbing way.

The Jewish student group and the Campus Ministry program brought a rabbi to speak on campus. This wasn't so unusual, but this rabbi happened to be a woman. This was new for me. Somehow, it fell to me to bring her to the first session and introduce her to the large gathering of people assembled to hear her speak. For some reason, she was late arriving on campus, so we were late getting to the hall. Everyone was very expectant. I had my little introduction speech all prepared, but I wasn't prepared for what actually came out of my mouth first. I said, "Thank you all for your patience. You've been waiting quite a while for this evening with Rabbi Geller. I know that I've been waiting for her my entire life."

Her presence that evening and over the next few days was stunning for me. I had one personal conversation with her, from which I realized that there were certain issues of Christian spirituality and theology with which I had become very comfortable, but that had no place in Jewish thought. I felt that a knife had just made a deep cut, severing a connection that had been so important for me. For so long, my worship life and my work and social lives were intricately woven around one another. I felt that I was losing my community, and this was very distressing.

Jackie says that in much the same way that she had originally wondered if she were forsaking her Judaism by going to ESR, she wondered if she were forsaking her love of Quakerism and her large Quaker community by embracing the reality that at root she is a Jew. This was not easily resolved in her mind. But she came to understand that such movement was inevitable, that her return to Judaism was not in spite of her Quaker travels, but largely because of them. The religious education, formal and informal, she has received among Quakers has given Jackie the theological and pastoral tools with which to move more deeply into her own center and to interpret her experience.

Choral Director

Following completion of her Master's in Divinity, she joined the music faculty of Earlham College. She was assistant to the head of the choral program. She particularly enjoyed working with the Chorale, a non-audition group of inexperienced singers. Many of them had not sung in a group before, and some did not read music. Four weeks into the school year, the group performed for Parents' Weekend at the College. After the performance, a Chorale parent told Jackie how wonderful it was to hear his son sing in a group. The father said, "I never knew he had it in him . . . thank you for bringing out a new boy." That experience reminded Jackie that success is not defined completely by how good a chorus sounds musically.

More Graduate School

The leading to work with choral groups continued to grow. Jackie realized that in order to develop her choral leadership ability, she needed more professional education. She attended two summer sessions at the Westminster Choir College in Princeton, New Jersey.

These sessions were inspirational. The first summer she took a course called Group Vocal Technique. The course gave her new vocabulary and insight in how to work with untrained singers. Jackie says, "The images and language and exercises addressed specific technical skills without using technical language . . . making it fun . . . making it accessible." This way of teaching was exactly what Jackie needed. "I was so excited," says Jackie. "I had no idea that something like this existed."

After a second summer at the Westminster Choir College, Jackie gained enough confidence to apply for the master's program there. It was at this point that Jackie needed financial help and applied to the Lyman Fund.

This step was next in her career, but it was more than that. It was the next step in her spiritual journey. She wrote in her application:

> I have often felt that I was somehow deficient or lazy because I couldn't foresee a "Five Year Plan" for my life. In seminary, I had no answer to the question, "What do you plan to do?" It still makes me uneasy to be confronted with such questions, but I am becoming increasingly familiar, even if not entirely comfortable, with the ambiguities of my patterns of growth. A friend recently offered me a more evolutionary model for my pattern of growth, reminding me that the way opens out around me more as I go than it does as I plan and calculate. As I move more into that way of perceiving, I find that even my

planning and calculating become freer and more receptive. When I have taken a misstep, there has often been a corrective to the path.

By traditional standards I think I have been slow to proceed and develop, perhaps even appearing to be undirected. But as I have reflected recently, I realize that while my path has been varied, even circuitous, it has not been random. There has been continuity and strong, consistent movement. There have been rich experiences and accumulating resources along the way, all of which continue to point me not only towards 'what' I am to do, but more fundamentally towards the Source and mode of that doing.

I feel that I am given more and more clarity about where I am at any particular moment, and insight into the promise of that kind of awareness. Curiously I feel I am also given more discernment into carrying out the practical details of following a leading, and more imagination about possible futures.

Relentless Recruiter

Jackie did well at her studies and has worked professionally directing choruses ever since. At George School, she leads a number of choruses, including one non-audition group of students, teachers, parents, and wider community members. Jackie says, "I am a relentless recruiter. I am shameless. I corner people at parties and ask them if they like to sing." Often the reply is, "Oh, I can't sing," or "You wouldn't want to hear me sing." I ask about their personal enjoyment, and they respond with a judgment about their ability.

On Parents' Weekend the mother of one of her choral students came for a parent conference. The mother spoke about how she had never been encouraged to sing as a child.

After the conference, Jackie invited this mother to step over to the piano and sing a few exercises. Although the woman hesitated, she tried it. Jackie helped her find her range and encouraged her to join the community chorus. "Tears came to her eyes," says Jackie. "She was so moved by the possibility that she could sing." This woman has joined the chorus.

This experience confirmed for Jackie how tender people feel about what it means to sing. She says, "I have become aware of what an intimate thing it is to sing and to listen to somebody sing. You are listening to somebody making their sounds." Sometimes it is a very simple thing which helps a singer. Jackie worked with one boy to open his mouth wider. This took time, but gradually he was able to do this. With encouragement and hard work, this boy became a soloist. Jackie says:

> Many people approach singing with real hesitancy and in some cases trepidation because they become so shy about their voices. I understand it. We are afraid to sound ugly. If, as a child, you are told not to sing, it is basically insinuated that there is some part of you that is ugly. It is like saying, "Wear a paper bag over your face." What control do you have as a child over the sound of your voice?

Jackie continues:

> I listen to people sing and it is amazing how many voice qualities there are. Everybody can blend in to make a very cohesive communal sound that really lifts the whole. I don't think I started with a vision of saving the world vocally, but I began to realize that singing is transforming. I love to see the look on people's faces when they realize that they can do it. The excitement in the group, I get tremendous energy from that.
>
> I believe that our relationship to our singing is more highly charged than our sense of ability in many other

areas. It cuts to the core of who we are. It is the sound we make. We are the instruments. In my fantasy world, we all recognize this as our birthright and gift, and we freely join our various sounds in song. The real story, however, is one of embarrassment and self-diminishment. Some draw a line between themselves and those in the realm of the competent elect. My work has focused on trying to draw those people back across that line, on helping them take the risk of group sound-making. It may be within the context of the most informal "sing-along," a more ritualized church congregational sing, or the most highly structured and disciplined rehearsing ensemble.

What helps Jackie is to step into the place that excites her. Recently, listening to one of her choruses, she thought,

That was really good. I am in the right place. I was listening to myself. I was listening to the group. I had a sort of out-of-body experience. I was saying, "I'm excited about this. This is fun. Some nice stuff is happening here. They are catching it, and I'm catching it." I felt like I'd arrived at a place that evening when I was making a difference.

Jackie has a number of practices that help her. One is to take time for centering herself before a rehearsal, time to be quiet. Jackie points out that rehearsals require such an outward focus that it is important to give herself the inward focus beforehand. She says:

I go sit in a quiet office and breathe. I get my head and my feet connected again. If I don't do that I notice a big difference. Conducting is very physical, it is almost like a dance. I work on getting the energy to go through my arms. I lie on the floor. I lift my arms and feel the weight of them. For conducting I want the limbs I use to be expressive and connected to my body and my mind and my head.

Return to Judaism

Living and working within Quaker community for 25 years have rekindled and reshaped Jackie's relationship to Judaism. She has grown closer to the traditions and observances, finding herself more and more moved by the beauty and depth of the language and spirituality. Recently, Jackie has begun to study the spoken Hebrew language, which she had learned to read as a child.

"The ironic thing is that my guidance back to Judaism comes from being among Quakers," she says:

> It was inevitable that the principle of the Inner Guide would eventually lead me to inner places that are true for me. The only real resolution was to continue to trust that I would continue to be led and the right balance would continue to be struck. So far I haven't had to abandon anything that bears real fruit.

There is a paradox in following the path of Judaism, and the path of Quakerism, which has a Christian heritage. Jackie recognizes the gift of each. She says:

> I have come to trust more and more in those things that seem paradoxical. I just hold them both, because then, what I need is shown to me. The paradoxical elements seem to complement each other, to regenerate each other. One helps me understand the other.

Jackie's life has come full circle. The woman raised in Judaism and nurtured as an adult through Quakerism is reclaiming the language and rituals of her youth. The small girl who enjoyed singing the Hebrew chants is now a choral director, calling forth the gift of sound and song in others. Staying faithful to leadings along the way, she has found and been found in the maturation of that life-long call.

XIII. AWAKENING

Pamela Meidell

Pamela Meidell

Beautiful words are not enough in establishing genuine world peace. We should instead embark on the difficult task of building an attitude of love and compassion within ourselves. Compassion is, by nature, peaceful and gentle, but it is also very powerful. I believe that its practice is the true source of happiness and of inner disarmament.

The Dalai Lama
(quoted from a letter to Pamela Meidell)

During the winter of 1992 I met Pamela Meidell at a Quaker vigil and protest at the Nevada Test Site, the testing ground for our government's nuclear weapons. Pamela was a staff person for Nevada Desert Experience, the organization which facilitated this event. Pamela's clear eyes, stately carriage, and calm manner struck me at once. Pamela has snow-white hair, unusual in a woman in her early forties. I learned Pamela was a Zen Buddhist priest. The two of us stood together in a silent vigil, holding between us a banner that said, "Healing the Earth; Healing Ourselves, One Planet, One Water, One Air, One Land, One People."

Pamela has the fertile imagination of a visionary combined with tremendous energy and stamina to bring visions into being. With her good sense of humor, she enjoys making wry comments. She is a walking encyclopedia of facts on nuclear issues.

Although Pamela is not a member of the Religious Society of Friends, she has affiliations with Friends. She often attends meeting for worship when visiting close friends who are Quakers. She has studied Quaker business practice, and intentionally uses it in facilitating meetings. Her peacemaking often brings her into cooperative action with Friends. Sometimes she describes herself as a Buddhist-Quaker.

Pamela's leading was to organize and lead a pilgrimage in 1995, at the time of the fiftieth anniversary of the dropping of the atom bomb in August of 1945. Pamela had faith that this pilgrimage could awaken people to the dangers of nuclear weapons. Joanna Macy has written in her book, **Despair and Personal Power in the Nuclear Age** *(p. 2)*, about the despair people are feeling since the dawn of the nuclear age. She says:

> *Until now, every generation throughout history lived with the tacit certainty that other generations would follow. Each assumed, without questioning, that its children and children's children and those yet unborn would carry on — to walk the same earth, un-*

> *der the same sky. Hardships, failures and personal*
> *death were ever encompassed in that vaster assur-*
> *ance of continuity. That certainty is now lost to us*
> *whether we work in the Pentagon or the peace move-*
> *ment. That loss, unmeasured and immeasurable, is*
> *the pivotal psychological reality of our time.*

Pamela's pilgrimage, the Atomic Mirror Pilgrimage, began
in Chimayo, New Mexico, then went on to Los Alamos, and
to the Trinity Site on the White Sands Missile Range where
the first atomic explosion in human history took place. The
pilgrims traveled by car, by foot, and by plane, the route of
those first bombs, to California, Hawaii, then to Hiroshima
on August 6 and Nagasaki on August 9 for the fiftieth anni-
versary ceremonies of the dropping of those two bombs three
days apart. The pilgrimage lasted three weeks, the same
span of time that elapsed between the explosion of the first
test atom bomb and the dropping of the A-bomb on
Hiroshima. The pilgrimage was designed to offer participants
a chance to retrace the journey of the bomb, to meet with
people along the way, and to have dialogue with them.

The Seed

A time of darkness began for Pamela Meidell when a nuclear
submarine base was built in Puget Sound near Pamela's
home in Seattle in 1977. When the base opened and the
first Trident submarine was to enter, anti-nuclear activists
arrived from all over the world. Pamela became involved.
As she learned more about nuclear weapons, she was horri-
fied. "I wanted to do something," she says. She decided to
offer her house as a base for visiting protesters but her husband could not agree to this. She says, "Something in me
closed down because of that." As their marriage of ten years
grew more difficult, Pamela and her husband divorced. Not
only was her marriage splitting up, but her primary Zen group

had also gone through a painful split. "I was in a slump," says Pamela, "a place of darkness."

A friend decided to help. She told Pamela the Dalai Lama was going to give an initiation called the "Kalachakra Initiation for World Peace." This was a very high initiation, usually quite secret, and in previous centuries given only to those practitioners who had undergone an extensive preparation. The Dalai Lama revealed he wanted to offer this initiation openly, because the world was in such a difficult state and the peace that came from this initiation was so needed. For Pamela, and others who had not undergone the preparation to receive it as an initiation, it would be offered as a "blessing." Pamela heard that the Dalai Lama was doing this initiation in Switzerland.

Pamela's friend said, "You should go to Switzerland." Pamela responded, "I can't afford it. I am barely making enough to live; I don't have any money." At that time Pamela was working as a temporary cleric at a real estate office. Pamela comments on how easy it is to listen to the negative voices inside. She says, "These voices will prevent you from doing anything in life if you listen to them." Her friend was persistent: "I'll find you the money," she said. She found a man who was willing to give Pamela a thousand dollars. Pamela did not even know him. Pamela told him she did not know if she could ever pay him back. The man replied, "It doesn't matter. When you can, give it to someone else." Pamela calls him "one of those angels on the path."

Her friend escorted her to the passport office and stood in line with her while she applied for her passport. An interesting synchronicity is that the passport Pamela received was dated July 16, 1985 and would expire ten years hence, on July 16, 1995, the date on which another pilgrimage would begin.

There were about a thousand people at the gathering in Switzerland. Pamela describes the blessing she received as "a seed planted deeply in a dark place which took time to germinate."

Folding Peace Cranes

When Pamela returned from Europe she moved to her parents' home in Oxnard, California. She lectured at the Asian Studies Institute at Pepperdine University. She did substitute teaching, ran a tutoring program, and took classes. She was feeling depressed. She continued her zazen meditation discipline and other related practices.

One spiritual discipline changed Pamela's life. This is the act of folding peace cranes. Pamela was driving her car along the Californian coastal highway one morning when she heard on the radio that children in Hiroshima and Nagasaki fold a thousand cranes before they are eighteen. The practice of folding cranes comes from the true story of a young Japanese girl from Hiroshima who was dying of leukemia. Her best friend brought her a golden origami crane in the hospital and told her the ancient belief that if someone folds 1,000 cranes she will get her wish. Little Sadako took heart from this story and began to fold her 1,000 cranes, wishing that she would get well. She folded 644 before she died. But on one of the last paper cranes she wrote the Japanese characters for peace. She gave it to her friend and said, "Peace crane, peace crane, I will write 'peace' on your wings and you will fly all over the world." After she died, her classmates folded the remaining cranes to make 1,000 and gave them to her parents. Children all over Japan heard this story and formed paper crane clubs to raise money to build a statue of Sadako in the Peace Park in Hiroshima, Japan. Every year people from all over the world bring garlands of 1,000 cranes to lay at this memorial. Because of Sadako, folding a thousand cranes has become an international symbol of world peace.

"I made this decision to fold a thousand cranes," says Pamela. "I folded four cranes every day." She picked out the colors for the cranes she folded that day based on her mood. At the same time she kept a journal of what was happening in the world. "The beauty of folding a crane touched me," she says. "It was a beautiful way to face an issue."

She folded cranes while she was on the telephone, on hold, waiting for someone. "I could fold a crane in two minutes," Pamela comments. Pamela is still folding cranes. Although she has folded over four thousand cranes, her goal is to fold ten thousand. She explains that in Buddhist belief, the "ten thousand things" means the infinite number of things in the material world; the number 10,000 is symbolic of an infinite number.

White Sands

A turning point in her life happened about two years after she had met the Dalai Lama. She had been folding her cranes each day. She walked into a card store and was drawn to a beautiful card, across the store. It was a desert scene. She walked over to it, looked at the back and read: "White Sands, New Mexico." Immediately she thought, "This is the place where the first atomic explosion took place. How could such a beautiful place be the entry point of such horror into our world?" The idea came to her consciousness: "I have to go to New Mexico and do something." She did not know what that "something" would be, but she knew she had to go where it all started. And she knew she had to take some cranes.

Less than a month later one of her friends phoned her and suggested the two of them could take a vacation together in New Mexico. Pamela accepted the invitation, telling her friend, "I just want to go to White Sands and do something, and then we can do whatever we want."

Pamela observes that once she had expressed the intention of going to New Mexico, the friend's invitation came within a month. She feels she is being led along the way by these mysterious happenings.

For Pamela there is a mystery around timing and around time. For instance, when the two women got to White Sands, they planned to have a small ceremony on the dunes. "We originally wanted to do the ceremony at dawn," says Pamela. "But all these things kept delaying it. It just seemed to be taking forever, like watching a film in slow motion." The two women talked about being tired and wondered whether they really had to do the ceremony now. Pamela says, "It was like somebody was holding onto my ankles."

In retrospect, Pamela sees this as the moment when she crossed a threshold that led to work she now does. She comments, "You do not usually recognize those moments when you are coming up on them. If you do recognize them in the moment, you are very lucky." Then she laughs and admits, "I didn't!"

First Pamela and her friend went to the museum. Then they had lunch in a picnic area. After lunch they lay down on the sand and fell asleep. Pamela says that this reminds her of a scene in the "Wizard of Oz." Dorothy and her companions are almost to the Emerald City when they walk through a field of poppies and fall asleep. You are right there on the verge and you say, "Let's do something else . . . have lunch . . . nap." When the two women woke up, Pamela asked her friend, "Do you think we really have to do this ceremony today?"

They both knew they were just putting it off. They walked out on the desert. They found a quiet spot at a sand dune. They drew a mandala in the sand. Then they took turns putting a crane in the circle for each year starting in 1945 when the first atom bomb was exploded. "We meditated on everything that died because of the nuclear age, people and animals and dreams that died." That ceremony marked a beginning of the next chapter of Pamela's life.

Having "done something," the two of them continued their vacation. They did the usual things, some shopping, some sight seeing, dinners out. But they kept running into places related to nuclear weapons. The two women were near Los Alamos, where scientists worked to create the atom bomb, so they went there. In a pueblo outside Albuquerque, they met people who had mined uranium. They happened to go by the National Atomic Museum near Albuquerque, so they visited that.

What struck Pamela was the paradox of coming upon these sites that symbolized to her destruction and death amidst the glorious desert scenery and the simple beauty of the pueblos. They were particularly struck by Chimayo, a tiny village where the inhabitants have been weavers for generations. The earth there is known for its healing qualities. Long ago it had been the site of a spring of healing waters. Gradually the spring dried up, leaving mud, and then dry earth. Pamela was moved when she heard about a Franciscan priest who for ten years brought the healing earth from Chimayo to the doorway of the Los Alamos National Laboratory 20 miles away.

The two women drove through the southwest, ending their "vacation" in Nevada at the Nevada Test Site. There they met the anti-nuclear activists of Nevada Desert Experience and decided to become involved. This vacation had became a pilgrimage, one so profoundly moving that these two women returned to repeat it annually for the next few years. It was the inspiration and the basis for the Atomic Mirror Pilgrimage. Within a year after this first trip to the Nevada Test Site, Pamela was invited to be on the board of Nevada Desert Experience.

Taking Her Vows

In 1992, Pamela took her vows as a Zen priest, in a private ritual that included a tea ceremony. She explained that Zen students all train together:

> I didn't train to become a priest; I trained together with other students. Gradually, as my practice continued and deepened, I felt led to make a stronger commitment, to take the next step. In my case, that

next step was to approach my teacher about taking priest vows.

Pamela's taking of vows was an important step in her spiritual journey. Taking vows is a way of expressing one's intention to wake up. Enlightenment is just being fully awake all the time. In Zen Buddhism there are two understandings of enlightenment. For some, it comes suddenly. For others, enlightenment comes as a gradual process, like a person who steps out into a misty day and gradually becomes wetter and wetter until the person becomes soaked.

Soon after she took her vows, a new phase of her life opened up. She was offered a newly-created job with Nevada Desert Experience. Pamela did not apply for the position; the board simply drafted her.

Death of Her Father

A year after Pamela accepted the job with Nevada Desert Experience, Pamela's father died suddenly. "I was very close to my father," says Pamela. Looking back, she thinks she poured the energy of her grief into her work. She was familiar with death and grief through her work with "Downwinders"—Mormons in Utah, and the Western Shoshone people whose land includes the test site. Many families had lost members to cancer from the exposure to radioactive fallout. Since the testing, these people had experienced an increase in cancer and death. Her reading and investigations showed that people all over the planet have suffered in this way from living too close to nuclear testing or nuclear accidents. She says:

> Now I knew from my own personal experience how terrible death is, even when it is a natural death. How much more terrible it is when death results from government lies or withheld information.

Branching Out on Her Own

Pamela threw herself into her work at Nevada Desert Experience, researching the nuclear history, publishing information, and hosting groups of people who came to vigil. "I can't remember how many times I was arrested," she says.

As the fiftieth anniversary of the atom bomb approached, the idea came to Pamela to offer a pilgrimage which would "open people's eyes to the truth." She thought that if she had been so unaware of this secret history and its events and effects on all of us, then perhaps other people were unaware of it as well. Pamela envisioned a pilgrimage from White Sands to Hiroshima and Nagasaki ending on the fiftieth anniversaries of the World War II bombings. Pamela wrote to the Dalai Lama for advice. He wrote a letter of encouragement and support and included these words:

> Beautiful words are not enough in establishing genuine world peace. We should instead embark on the difficult task of building an attitude of love and compassion within ourselves. Compassion is, by nature, peaceful and gentle, but it is also very powerful. I believe that its practice is the true source of happiness and of inner disarmament.

At this point in Pamela's journey, her vision was like a very young plant that had begun to grow down in the earth but had not yet come to the surface. It was but a nudge inside Pamela. The next step, to bring this vision into reality, would require an enormous effort, changing the entire direction of Pamela's life.

Pamela's job at Nevada Desert Experience was meaningful work and provided her with a salary. She says, "It would have been very easy for me to just keep doing what I was doing, but it was the idea of the pilgrimage that had grabbed hold of me. I had to be faithful to that somehow." She had to leave her job.

This was a time of extreme loneliness. She remembers people saying they thought the whole idea was kind of foolish. Friends pointed out that she had a good paying job and she was doing important work. Yet she was drawn to her vision. "These things you do alone," she says. "These are the things in life that you need to do or else you are not living. If it is not alive, why are you doing it?"

One factor that allows Pamela to follow her inner nudges is the fact that she is single. She has no husband and children to consider. She is free to put her energy into following the Spirit wherever she feels nudged to go. Yet to do this requires a great deal of faith.

Pamela remarks at how easy it is to become discouraged with one's projects when one can't seem to get anything going. She loves a story that Thich Nhat Hahn tells in his book, *Living Buddha; Living Christ.* St. Francis is walking in an almond grove. He is very discouraged and cries to God in despair. Suddenly the almond trees all burst into bloom. Pamela knows that sometimes we must be patient while the project is in the dormant stage, like a tree in winter. We must hold the vision. We must have faith that one day our little sapling will burst into bloom.

Although most people were not encouraging, Pamela had one close friend who believed in this vision. Sometimes that is all it takes—one steady voice of encouragement. This friend knew about the Lyman Fund and encouraged Pamela to apply for a grant. Pamela received a grant to free up half her work time for planning the pilgrimage. Along with the grant, board members of the fund promised to hold Pamela's vision in the Light. Pamela states, "This support really gave me the confidence and courage to carve out the time for the pilgrimage."

Pamela named the pilgrimage the "Atomic Mirror." The image comes from the Greek myth of Medusa, the gorgon with hair of writhing snakes. Every warrior who tried to slay her turned to stone upon looking at her. Only Perseus, who had received a mirrored shield as a gift from the gods, was able to approach her by looking at her reflection in his shield rather than directly at her. By gazing in the Atomic Mirror, people would be able to take in the horror of nuclear disasters and be able to act.

Although Pamela had initial support, the next period of time was extremely challenging. How would she find the people to join her on the pilgrimage? Who would go? Pamela's faith was sorely tested. "I wondered if the whole thing might come crashing down," recalls Pamela.

Fortunately she met two women who joined her efforts. Edie Hartshorne, a musician, and Mayumi Oda, a visual artist, worked with Pamela to create a performance piece related to the nuclear age. The three of them traveled and performed this piece, gathering potential pilgrims and raising funds for the pilgrimage.

Edie played, in turn, Japanese wooden flutes, Tibetan bowls, and a Koto, a beautiful large Japanese stringed instrument. Mayumi and Pamela became the voices of people who had been affected in powerful ways by some aspect of the nuclear age. Mayumi's paintings of benevolent female guardians and goddesses provided a visual environment for the piece.

Pamela and her friends worked hard to raise money and recruit potential pilgrims. In order to make the pilgrimage accessible to people with limited amounts of time and money, Pamela set it up so that people could be free to join in or leave as they could. This meant a person could join in for a weekend or a few days.

Planning became a nightmare. "Logistics are one of my weaknesses," Pamela says. She came close to despair a number of times over arranging for housing, figuring out how to feed everyone, how to arrange to get from place to place. Pamela struggled to take care of these details. In the end she did barely have the required number of airline passengers to Japan in order to have her own way paid.

Pilgrimage Begins in Chimayo

A hundred pilgrims, friends, and relatives gathered in Chimayo on July 14, two days before the ceremony at Trinity test site. Pamela describes the village:

> We drove into this dusty square. There is an outdoor chapel with stone benches outside it. There are huge cottonwood trees and there is a little creek running by.

A Jewish woman rabbi was one of the pilgrims. The rabbi connected today's threat of nuclear holocaust with the Jewish holocaust during World War II. Pamela and the rabbi led the opening ceremony. Gifts were laid on the altar, gifts the pilgrims had been given to carry to Hiroshima and Nagasaki. The pilgrims were planning to carry the four elements, earth, water, air, and fire. Earth from Chimayo. Sacred water from Mt. Shasta in California, sister mountain to Mount Fuji in Japan. Air was represented by a gift of owl feathers from the Umatilla Tribe near Hanford, Washington where the plutonium was made for the Nagasaki bomb. The Umatilla people told Pamela, "We want to send something beautiful as a gift, because fifty years ago we sent such a terrible thing to them."

Fire came from Hiroshima. A Japanese pilgrim had carried the flame from Hiroshima in a small hand warmer. It is a flask with fuel in it, the kind often used by Japanese fishermen. This man was five years old when he saw the bomb drop out of the sky. He called to his mother to come out and look, and that is why his mother survived. The house was completely crushed.

The pilgrims found it was impractical to carry the flame on their journey. So they brought the flame to Los Alamos and gave it to the people working at the United States government facility. Symbolically they returned the fire of the bomb back to its source.

That night the pilgrims met at the Fuller Lodge at the Los Alamos facility with staff people from there, and community members who had organized the evening. One teenager told Pamela she was the daughter of someone who worked on the Manhattan Project, the original Los Alamos project that created the bomb. About sixty people sat around four sides of a square, facing the center. Each person had a chance to speak once, to express what was on their hearts. Pamela was touched by the trust and intimacy. "People were listening to each other," she says. In communities along the way, such as in Las Vegas, or San Francisco, the pilgrims were hosted by local groups.

Japan

The pilgrimage continued, stopping at many places, including the Nevada Test Site, Lawrence Livermore National Laboratory, Pearl Harbor, Hawaii, and Japan. At each place the pilgrims offered their gifts and prayers and tried to have dialogues with people there. The last days were in Nagasaki, Japan.

Here the pilgrims stayed in a 12th-century Buddhist temple. Outside the temple hung a huge wooden carp. In the early morning a monk announced the dawn by beating on the carp with a wooden mallet. This temple was one of a dozen temples that stand in a row at the base of the mountain. Pamela and her friends went to each one, offering prayers, then walked up the mountain to where they had a good view of the whole city with the harbor beyond.

Wonderful moments characterized the time in Nagasaki. On the way down to the harbor, Pamela and the pilgrim who was a rabbi stopped at a small shop. On the wall was a poster of Anne Frank. The rabbi told the shop keeper how touched she was to see this symbol of the Jewish holocaust. The shopkeeper took the poster off the wall and gave it to the rabbi.

Another touching event was when two of the pilgrims, a German nuclear physicist and the American Jewish rabbi, quietly decided to take a day of fasting together. It has been those small, yet profound, experiences that have meant the most to Pamela.

The pilgrims hoped to have a meeting with the mayor of Nagasaki to present him with the earth, water, and owl feathers they had carried from Chimayo. But the mayor, of course, was extremely busy during this period. Pamela and the other pilgrims wondered how they could possibly arrange a meeting.

One of the pilgrims was from Okinawa. He alerted the group that there would be a group of paddlers in canoes arriving at the dock that evening, having paddled canoes from Okinawa to Nagasaki. The pilgrims went down to the dock and found the mayor there to meet the paddlers. It was a perfect opportunity to present their gifts to the mayor, along with a message of hope for world peace. Miraculously, a way had opened for them. This was a marvelous climax to the pilgrimage.

Does the Leading End?

The Atomic Mirror Pilgrimage was over. At least Pamela thought so. But when you go on a spiritual journey, one path often leads into another. Pamela was not going to have a rest, at least not for a while. The next step revealed itself even before Pamela's feet left the soil of Japan. Janet Bloomfield, a British pilgrim, expressed the hope that Pamela might join in a similar pilgrimage through Britain, possibly the following April, to commemorate the tenth anniversary of the accident at Chernobyl in 1986. Of course Pamela agreed.

Another significant connection happened on the way home, when she stopped in Hawaii. She met Kilali Alailima, who worked for American Friends Service Committee there. This woman later would become Pamela's colleague in coordinating the conference of the International Abolition 2000 network to eliminate nuclear weapons, a conference which would take place two years later in Tahiti.

Pamela told Kilali about the pilgrimage and how they brought healing earth from Chimayo. Kilali responded, "Oh, do you mean this?" Reaching into her purse, Kilali pulled out a wallet in which she carried earth from Chimayo. Then Kilali told Pamela an amazing story. The previous July she and her husband had been traveling in New Mexico when Kilali felt the urge to visit the Four Corners area of the Southwest. It was July 14. The couple drove to Chimayo and visited the sanctuary. Kilali stood in the chapel and prayed that when she reached Hawaii she would work to stop the French nuclear testing in the Pacific. Kilali and her husband noticed a group of people were having some kind of ceremony. After a while the couple drove on. Kilali did not know it at the time, but this was the opening ceremony of the Atomic Mirror Pilgrimage.

Pamela notes with awe the synchronicity that drew Kilali to Chimayo on the day the pilgrimage began. "To me this is a very profound one." Pamela has been amazed at such synchronicities. She comments:

> I think when I first went to White Sands, I stepped over a threshold into some territory that is always unknown, but where things are always coming together in ways I cannot explain.

The pilgrimage had connected Pamela to many companions. They gave her hope and encouragement. It meant a lot to her to have found these companions on the journey. Although most of the people with whom she had bonded lived far away, she could still connect with them by telephone, letters, and electronic mail.

Pamela came to visit me after the pilgrimage. She loves ceremony and had planned one for me because of the part the Lyman Fund played in her pilgrimage. She arrived at my home carrying a large pottery bowl wrapped in a shawl. The bowl contained the earth and seeds from the places she visited on the pilgrimage. She suggested a ceremony just for the two of us. It was a beautiful day. We sat at my picnic table outside my home near the ocean. We took time in a silent prayer of gratitude. She carefully folded an origami pouch into which she placed earth and seeds from all the places she had been. It was a beautiful ceremony and I was profoundly touched. She let me know that our fund had participated in the pilgrimage in some small and yet meaningful way.

Crash

Pamela continued to work intensively. She joined a pilgrimage and went through England, Scotland and Wales. As soon as the British pilgrimage was completed, she worked with Kilali on the Pacific conference in Tahiti, which included over one hundred anti-nuclear activists from all over the world.

Pamela had kept up an amazing pace for a number of years. She has much more stamina than most people. But even Pamela has her limits. At the end of the conference in Tahiti she was very tired. It was then that she felt a tightening, like a fist, around her heart. She went to see her doctor. He declared her heart was fine; she was simply suffering from stress. Pamela's body was telling her something. For the next six months, Pamela took a break.

Spiritual Practice

Whether or not Pamela is on the road or at home, she takes time for morning spiritual grounding. Pamela's current spiritual practice is to begin each morning with sitting meditation (zazen), followed by prayer and yoga. Then she makes a pot of tea and writes a few pages in her journal—associative writing—before breakfast. Over breakfast, she reads her favorite comic strip, Sylvia, then turns to the editorial and other pages, clipping out pertinent articles.

Dream work is also important to Pamela. She keeps a pad of paper near her bed. In the night if she has a dream, she writes a few notes on the pad. In the morning she tries to read them, and remember the dream, so she can write it down. Periodically she reviews her dreams, looking for recurring themes and images. Sometimes she draws the images in her journal.

Although some of the particular disciplines may change, Pamela has been doing spiritual practice each morning for years. She says, "I believe that this inner foundation of spiritual work grounds my outward service in the world."

It's the Faces of the People

I asked Pamela to consider her path over the past few years. What is it that keeps her going? What gives the pilgrimages so much meaning for her? "It's the faces of the people," she responds.

> I keep seeing the faces of all the people in the communities where we stayed on the pilgrimages. Small groups of people who are keeping the faith alive, people who are resisting nuclear weapons and nuclear power and trying to live in such a way as not to be dependent upon that kind of security.

One of her special memories is staying with a family in the middle of Wales whose nine-year-old daughter wrote a letter to the President of France asking him not to resume nuclear testing. Another favorite memory is staying with four women in a peace camp near Menwith Hill spy base. One of these women had lived in the American southwest and cooked up chili for the pilgrims made with chili peppers from Chimayo.

Pamela has made friends with people from all over the world. "I have met wonderful, funny, dedicated people," she says. "You can't do this work for a long time without a sense of humor. We have had some wacky times."

"As we travel from place to place, we carry the stories from previous places," says Pamela.

> We are living letters. We are telling stories of hope to people who can sometimes feel very isolated. There is something that feels very ancient to me about this. These people might receive this information through a fax or literature, but we are making a personal connection.

Pamela's own personal inner journey has come a long way as well. Looking back, she comments, "When I first started doing this work I was bringing bad news." She was alerting people to the terrible effects of nuclear testing. Since she has met so many people all over the world who are working to promote a nuclear-free world, Pamela now sees herself as "the bearer of good news as well." Her life has become richer than she could have imagined. She says, "I feel profoundly grateful."

XIV. GOD'S TIMING

Barbara Bazett

Barbara Bazett

Neither pray I for these alone, but for them also
which shall believe on me through their word;
That they all may be one; as thou, Father, art in me,
and I in thee, that they also may be one in us:
that the world may believe that thou hast sent me.

St. John 17: 20-21 (KJV)

*B*arbara Bazett meets me in the comfortable little upstairs library of Woodbrooke, a Quaker study center in Birmingham, England, where we both have come to a large gathering of Friends. Barbara has come from her home in Vancouver. She is short and stocky, with a warm, outgoing manner, and she gives me a cheery greeting as we sit down to talk. She seems delighted to be interviewed and readily answers my questions, speaking quickly and easily.

Barbara's most recent leading has been ecumenical work on a global scale. She is a Quaker representative from Canadian Yearly Meeting to the World Council of Churches. She has served for seven years as the only Friends representative on the Central Committee which meets once every year in a different country each time.

Barbara's story illustrates how God works in the world and God's timing of that work. In Barbara's childhood a seed was planted, a yearning for international and ecumenical harmony. This remained dormant for decades. It was long after her children were grown when Barbara was called to represent Quakers on the World Council of Churches. Even then, what seemed to be required of her was patience and prayer. In her third year she was dramatically nudged by the Spirit. Most importantly, when God called, she was available.

Thomas Kelly writes in Testament of Devotion *(p. 118),* about living in guidance:

> *Under the silent, watchful eye of the Holy One we all are standing, whether we know it or not. And in that Center, in that holy Abyss where the Eternal dwells at the base of our being, our programs, our gifts to Him, our offerings of duties performed are again and again revised in their values. Many of the things we are doing seem so important to us. We haven't been able to say No to them, because they seemed*

so important. But if we center down, as the old phrase goes, and live in that holy Silence which is dearer than life, and take our life program into the silent places of the heart, with complete openness, ready to do, ready to renounce according to His leading, then many of the things we are doing lose their vitality for us. I should like to testify to this, as a personal experience, graciously given. There is a re-evaluation of much that we do or try to do, which is done for us, and we know what to do and what to let alone.

Kelly continues (p. 124):

When we say Yes or No to calls for service on the basis of heady decisions, we have to give reasons, to ourselves and to others. But when we say Yes or No to calls, on the basis on inner guidance and whispered promptings of encouragement from the Center of our life, or on the basis of a lack of any inward "rising" of that life to encourage us in the call, we have no reason to give, except one—the will of God as we discern it. Then we have begun to live in guidance. And I find He never guides us into an intolerable scramble of panting feverishness. The Cosmic Patience becomes, in part, our patience, for after all God is at work in the world. It is not we alone who are at work in the world, frantically finishing a work to be offered to God.

Life from the Center is a life of unhurried peace and power. It is simple. It is serene. It is amazing. It is triumphant. It is radiant. It takes no time, but it occupies all our time. And it makes our life programs new and overcoming. We need not get frantic. He is at the helm. And when our little day is done we lie down quietly in peace, for all is well.

The Seed

To understand Barbara's passion for ecumenical work one must go back to her childhood. Born in 1930, Barbara's first five years were spent in Bangkok. She says:

> In those days the expatriates were seven hundred in number. It was a very gracious time with big houses and large servants' quarters. I was the first child in our family. We had a staff of about thirty servants, Thai people (called "Siamese" in those days), and a Sikh who was both chauffeur and night watchman. There were Chinese house boys and all their families. My father was a merchant and had Chinese merchant friends who came to the house. I had my own "ayah" (nanny), a loving, gentle young woman. She was always there for me. I have been looking for someone like her ever since.

Barbara laughs as she talks about this.

> I used to run down to the servants' quarters because I was bilingual. I would chatter away in Thai with this group. They were all very loving . . . you know how people are with small children, especially in Asia. So the world was beautiful. The sun shone. All these different colors were loving and supportive people. And that is how the world should be. I realized later in life that this was the root of my desire to work with the World Council of Churches. I wanted to enable people to get to know one another better, to work together, and to love one another and realize they were one human family—children of one God.

Youth in England

Barbara's family returned to England in 1935. The family attended the Church of England (Anglican/Episcopalian);

Barbara had friends who belonged to different Christian churches. As a young girl, she used to go to church with her family in the morning, visit with her friends in the afternoon and go to evening service in her friends' churches. Barbara says:

> I experienced God as present no matter which Christian church I went to. I got very hurt when I heard one church person running down another church. It was like making rude remarks about my family. It pained me in my heart; it literally gave me a pain.

Barbara did not find the Anglican service relevant. Even at age ten or eleven she found the words got in the way of her being able to worship. She recalls her impressions of the service:

> You stood up to sing and then sat down to listen and then stood up for praise, but there was no place where you could hear God. It seemed to me what I heard in the Gospel stories bore no relation to what I saw going on. I objected to being sermonized. I complained to my parents and said that I didn't want to go, so my parents let me stay home and fix Sunday lunch.

Young Barbara admits she was a very bright kid. Even at a young age she loved to read newspaper stories. She knew the House of Lords was opposed to the church taking stands on social issues. When she was about ten years old she heard Archbishop William Temple, a church leader who would become one of the founders of the World Council of Churches, speaking on the radio. What he said touched her heart. He spoke of his dream of the churches working together and how we (Christians) were called to be together and how important that was. This was during World War II years, before the creation of World Council of Churches in 1948. The Archbishop spoke with passion. Barbara recalls:

> I found it very exciting. He was saying what I had wanted to hear. When I heard him, my heart burned

within me, as the disciples' hearts must have burned on the road to Emmaus (when the risen Christ appeared to the disciples, Luke 24:32). Inside me I remember feeling warmth, and light, and recognition. This church leader was saying what I really believed in. That talk planted a seed in me.

Drawn to Friends

When she was a child, Barbara had heard about Friends through reading a novel in which the protagonist sits in the silence of a Quaker meeting for worship. At her school she learned about Elizabeth Fry, a Quaker who went into prisons to help prisoners and institute reform. She read biographies of other Quakers. Barbara was drawn by the fact that the Quakers she read about lived their faith seven days a week.

It was not until Barbara had finished college and was married that she thought about becoming a Quaker herself. She responded to a notice in the newspaper and received the literature.

She remembers reading the material and thinking, "This is great, absolutely splendid!" But she postponed going to meeting. She put the material in the bottom drawer of her dresser. She says, "It beamed at me for two years and finally I said, 'Oh, alright.' " The very first time she attended a Quaker meeting she felt, "I have come home."

Drawn into Spiritual Guidance

The next chapter of Barbara's life story began when the family, including four children, moved to Vancouver in 1966. Soon after this her husband left and the couple was divorced. Barbara supported her family by teaching at the University and the Community College.

A few years after her divorce she married an engineer, a committed Anglican, who was father of two young children. As an ecumenical family, they took all six children to Quaker meeting one Sunday and church the next.

Over the years Barbara began to be aware of people coming to her with spiritual questions. This even happened in her thirties. The first time she had attended Canadian Yearly Meeting, an older woman, known as a "weighty Friend," came up to her and said, "Can we go for a walk?" The next thing the woman said was, "I've lost my faith." Barbara comments, "I had all my antennae out and was praying hard and listening hard (to God) at the same time as I was listening to her."

When that kind of situation kept recurring, Barbara knew she needed to learn from people with experience in spiritual direction. She began to meet with a Catholic priest and took a course from an Anglican nun. She attended a weekend at Pendle Hill in Spiritual Friendship and began a spiritual friendship with another Canadian Quaker. This friendship has continued until now and is a very important part of Barbara's life.

Barbara works very hard at what she does. After the workshop on spiritual friendship, Barbara started a program for this among Friends in Canada when she got home. Barbara thrives on learning and then teaching what she has learned, making this information available to others. She has a lot of perseverance.

World Council Comes to Vancouver

When Barbara heard that the World Council of Churches was going to have the 1983 General Assembly in Vancouver, she was thrilled. The General Assembly, in which representatives from all over the world come together for two weeks, only happens every seven years. She had not forgotten the nudge she had felt at age ten when she heard Archbishop

Temple on the radio. Now at age 53, Barbara felt the nudge again. "It was like having the Kingdom of Heaven visit your back yard." She volunteered to help and was appointed chair of the host program committee to prepare for the five thousand people expected. Barbara's job was to devise a program that would put all the delegates in touch with church people in Vancouver. It turned out to be a big job. Barbara worked with others to enlist 1,500 volunteers to write to all the delegates ahead of time to make them feel welcome. Some invited delegates to come early and stay in their homes for a few days to recover from jet-lag and to be their "friend away from home." Barbara spent three years setting this up.

By the time the General Assembly of the World Council of Churches happened, Barbara decided to attend the meetings as a visitor. The Assembly lasted two weeks. Barbara attended all the meetings and she loved every moment of it. By the end of it, she was hooked. She says:

> I was so excited, I reported to Canadian Yearly Meeting that I intended to go to the next Assembly seven years later, in 1991, and save up the money even if I had to take in laundry to do it.

Training to Do Spiritual Nurture

Meanwhile Barbara felt the need to train more intentionally for doing spiritual nurture. She heard about two different courses, one at an ecumenical theological school in Vancouver and another one at Pendle Hill, a Quaker center near Philadelphia. Obviously the Vancouver school would be less expensive and more convenient. Barbara was living with her second husband and two of their children at the time. Her husband preferred that she attend the school in Vancouver. Barbara brought the discernment question to her spiritual director. The spiritual director reflected back what she heard:

When you talk about the one in Vancouver there is no life in you. But when you talk about the other one, the energy and life is present in your face; you are all lit up.

The director also pointed out that Barbara was becoming involved in ecumenical work. For this, it would be important to get a better grounding in her own tradition.

Pendle Hill

Barbara kept holding the question open for discernment. What she wanted was the best training for becoming a spiritual director. Barbara attended a conference in Indiana. At the conference she saw a slide show about Pendle Hill. What she saw confirmed that this was the place she needed to go for training.

There was still the problem of finding funding. At the conference she heard about our fund and applied for a grant to cover the three months term at Pendle Hill. Barbara describes the discernment process thus:

Pendle Hill had been like a little dot in the corner of my mental TV screen. When I first heard about it, it was like an express train coming down a track so that the front of the train filled the whole screen. It was clearly something to pay attention to. I went.

Husband's Response

One of the challenges facing Barbara was the response of her husband to her taking time away from home. She says:

He did not understand why I wanted to go. He did not believe in leadings. He did not believe God told people to do anything. He said it was an unfair argument to use in any dispute because how could he argue against God?

Barbara took her husband's concern into her prayers. It was difficult to leave him when he did not want her to go. Yet she felt God was leading her to go to Pendle Hill. She was clear. At that time the two children living at home were old enough to take care of themselves. Barbara filled the freezer with precooked meals and took off for Pendle Hill. Her husband was unhappy while she was away. She felt this when she telephoned home. She says, "It was like this for years when I went to yearly meeting or anything." While her husband's attitude was not supportive, Barbara continued to follow her leadings. She explains she had learned in her first marriage that it did not work to give up one's own spiritual path. She says:

> In my first marriage I lived through my husband's work and career. That is what I was raised to do. That is what we were all taught. It is still inside of all of us. I have to fight on the inside as well as on the outside to stand up for my own individuality and be a whole person so I can bring that to the relationship. It's hard work.

Barbara relies on her spiritual friend and her faith community to support her in that effort. She says, "That is why we live and work in community; we need the community to validate what we are hearing and to encourage us to keep going."

It was during this term at Pendle Hill that Barbara heard she had been nominated by Canadian Yearly Meeting of Friends to serve on the World Council of Churches. Being appointed a delegate meant she had her way paid to go to the General Assembly in Australia.

Only then did Barbara understand that the primary reason she had to be at Pendle Hill was not to train for spiritual direction, as she had thought, but rather to ground herself in her own faith so she could better represent Friends at the World Council of Churches. She also understood that her leading to do spiritual direction was on hold for the time being. Barbara comments:

> I have found this many times in my life: God gets me
> to a place where he needs me to be by whatever
> means he can get me there, and then I find out when
> I am there why I am really there.

World Council of Churches

Barbara traveled to the 1991 General Assembly to Canberra,
Australia, as a delegate from Canadian Yearly Meeting. In
Canberra, a way opened for Barbara to sit on the Central
Committee which meets once a year.

When Barbara was asked if she ever had feelings of inad-
equacy when meeting with the weighty religious leaders of
churches around the world, she responded:

> I spoke with (my spiritual friend) about it. She told
> me that a sense of inadequacy in a call should not
> stop you because basically it is based in pride. You
> just have to trust God. So you don't look as good as
> you would like to look; God will get the work done
> through you; don't worry about it.

Barbara relies on holding on to the continuing inner word
that keeps coming, "Yes . . . This is what you are to do." She
says, "I hold onto the sense of joy and rightness in being
there and the sense that this is the right place." Her monthly
meeting appointed a support group of three people who
would meet and pray with her before she left, pray for her
while she was there, and then would see her when she came
home. "That was very helpful," she reports.

The meeting days on the Central Committee were long,
beginning at nine in the morning and going non-stop until
nine-thirty at night. Barbara says, "I knew I had to be there,
but I didn't know why. I did not know what I was to do. I am
not very good, temperamentally, with waiting around. The
first session I just listened. She says:

If you open your mouth you are taken as speaking for all the Quakers in the world and for Canada, so you have to be very careful what you say. You are given three minutes in which to say it before the buzzer goes off.

One thing that has helped Barbara to stay centered in this work has been to stick to doing certain spiritual disciplines every day. She starts her day with spiritual practices. She says:

I don't always achieve this, but I get up half an hour early in the morning and practice the Buddhist breath prayer and awareness meditation for half an hour. Thich Nhat Hahn writes about it in *The Miracle of Mindfulness.*

After that I say the Lord's Prayer with gestures. At the World Council meetings everyone says the Lord's Prayer in their mother tongue. You hear this murmur all around and you are part of the family of God. It struck me one day that this prayer is going on twenty-four hours a day as the world turns and moves into the light, somebody will be saying the Lord's Prayer. So I am not saying it, I am just slipping into the saying of it.

(At this point in the interview Barbara, always the teacher, took time to teach me body movements to use with the Lord's Prayer.)

At the Central Committee Meeting the second year Barbara again did not find herself called to speak much. Both years she was surprised how much she loved all these people she did not know very well. "There was a sense of love that was not mine, much bigger than I would have, flowing through me for the entire time."

Barbara found the people on the committee to be very beautiful. They were all trying to hear each other, trying to find a way forward together, committed very deeply to their

Christianity. They were pouring themselves out during this time to be there and to do this, all searching for God's will. Barbara says that if you talk with any of them and touch a certain button, you hear their underlying passion that comes from Jesus' words:

> Neither pray I for these alone, but for them also which shall believe on me through their word; that they all may be one; as thou, Father, art in me, and I in thee, that they also may be one in us: that the world may believe that thou hast sent me.

St. John 17:20-21 (KJV)

Barbara loves these words. She says:

> Once you have heard that you cannot unhear it. Once you have heard that as a true call, you can't pretend you haven't. Because it rings very loudly all the time. That sense of togetherness. My heart hungers for that, to enable that, to be a part of that, to see it happen.

So Barbara sat in the first two meetings and love poured through her and she thought, "Is this what I am supposed to do, uphold them in prayer and love them?"

She checked this with an experienced Jesuit and he said, "That is probably the most important thing that is happening there. If that is all you do for seven years, that's fine."

Johannesburg

The third year was a different story. The Central Committee met in Johannesburg, South Africa shortly after apartheid was eliminated and Nelson Mandela became president. Barbara says:

> I had always been interested in South Africa. Being British I felt responsible for what we had done there and for apartheid, which had happened while we were

there. It has always been on my heart. I was over-joyed to go there.

Many black African church leaders who had been tortured and jailed were there from the South African Council of Churches. They were talking reconciliation, love and peace. The first night was an opening worship with the theme of "The Light shines in the darkness and the darkness has never put it out." (Good News Bible, John 1:5)

Barbara described the service:

The choir from Soweto came dancing down the aisle, singing and clapping. Then they stood and sang the African National Anthem, "God Bless Africa." They sang with every fiber of their being because now they were free people in their own country, full citizens.

As Barbara related the story, her voice cracked and tears rolled down her cheeks.

Bishop Stanley Mugabo, a Methodist black African Bishop from Johannesburg, preached. He said that the world knew where the churches stood on racism, that racism was wrong. Now it was time that the churches of the world turn their attention to the last great evil, violence and war.

Barbara says, "When he said it, it was like a spear piercing my heart. I can still feel it going right in. I knew that I had to do this." The next morning she met in the lobby the representative from the Church of the Brethren, a peace church that often works with Friends on peace issues. He had heard the same call, and asked Barbara, "Do you think we can do this?"

She responded, "I'm sure we can. This has to be done." Barbara went off to the British Friend who was on the World Council of Churches staff there in charge of peace concerns to ask how to go about this. At the coffee break Barbara and the Church of the Brethren representative drafted a proposal for the Program to Overcome Violence. They brought it to the staff person at lunch, and she encouraged them to take it to the General Secretary, Konrad Raiser. Raiser, a pacifist, was very keen on it and told them to which committee to take it. Many people then worked to see that the proposal went forward. He went to the committee meeting himself to put his weight behind it. When a proposal comes to the floor, the delegates vote by holding up orange cards. Barbara recalls, with tears in her eyes, the vote on this proposal.

> You turned around in this big auditorium, and it looked like a field of butterflies because every card was up and being waved. The tears poured down my face because it had happened. The proposal passed unanimously.

It was a miracle. To get a proposal for a whole new program onto the agenda of an international meeting was amazing. All the agenda items are planned months ahead. Barbara comments:

> This was God moving. In a sense it had nothing to do with me. I was there in the right place at the right time. I was from a small church without another agenda. If I had come with an agenda, I would have been too busy to do this. I was open and free. That is why God had me there.

Does the Leading Ever End?

Barbara's seven-year term as a representative ended with the next General Assembly in 1998. She did not go. Her husband had become frail with severe congestive heart failure. Her glaucoma had given her trouble. She had to undergo an operation to heal a detached retina. She felt the need to stay closer to home.

> It is becoming increasingly clear to me that now is the time to practice spiritual direction more formally.

I will put my name on a list of people who are willing to do this. Then I will work with people from any tradition who wish to come. This continues my ecumenical experience.

Reflecting upon her experience in the World Council, Barbara says, "I feel I have accomplished part of what I was here to do." She speaks about feeling a sense of fulfillment, a sense of joy, and of freedom. "Ego is not tied up in it," she says. "It is really nothing to do with me." While it has been a joy for her, it has also been a tremendous amount of work. She says:

I'm burned out. It is good to lay it down because I would not be the right person to continue it. I am tired and jaded. If I were to continue I would be outrunning my guide.

This is a transition time. I have a sense of it coming to an end. This is a clear sense. I can trust it. But there is an ache. At the last Central Committee I was aware that I would most likely not see these people again. They have become like family. There is a grief in perhaps not seeing them again. Because the work is not mine, I can see God has placed in position the people to carry it forward, in whose faithfulness and ability I can trust. So I can hand it over. I can feel that I have laid down my bit, and they can pick it up and run with it.

CONCLUSION

Charlotte Fardelmann

The kingdom of heaven is like to a grain of mustard seed, which a man took, and sowed in his field: Which indeed is the least of all seeds: but when it is grown, it is the greatest among herbs, and becometh a tree, so that the birds of the air come and lodge in the branches thereof.

Matthew 13:31-32 (KJV)

The nudge to write this book was a leading. I'm thankful to have had this opportunity. Not only has this experience brought me closer to people, but it has taught me many lessons.

The most important lesson is the primacy of one's relationship with the One who leads. However we keep that connection, keep open to Divine guidance, this is the key to living our leadings. It is only through God's grace that we are able to plunge along the often obscure route of one's spiritual journey. The spiritual practices vary, but the faithfulness required is a constant.

Jesus says:

> Abide in me, and I in you. As the branch cannot bear fruit of itself, except it abide in the vine; no more can ye, except ye abide in me. I am the vine, ye are the branches: He that abideth in me, and I in him, the same bringeth forth much fruit: for without me ye can do nothing.

> John 15:4 (KJV)

Not only is each of these people rooted in his or her own prayer life, but also supported by the prayers of others. I've been humbled by the prayer support for this book. Some intercessary prayer is known and acknowledged with gratitude, but there is much more prayer of which the recipient is not aware. We who travel under the care of the Spirit swim in a sea of prayer.

These stories are rooted in the ground of life experience. What happened during childhood very often creates the springboard for a leading. In God's economy, nothing is wasted. A person who has suffered may yearn to make the world better for others coming along. The path to which one is led may be counter-cultural; one may find oneself marching to a different drummer.

These stories are full of giving gracefully and also receiving with grace. I've learned that when one gives in the right spirit, it is a gift to the "receiver." If one receives in the right spirit, it is a gift to the "giver." In this interaction, there is no way to discern who is the giver and who is the receiver. Giving and receiving, like yin and yang, do not happen one after the other, but simultaneously. There is a glow about such interactions that blesses everyone around them.

The biggest mystery is how God's grace works. Synchronicities happen, signs of when God chooses to remain anonymous. Just when a person thinks the money is going to run out, an unexpected windfall appears. Our job is to keep the faith and hold the vision. We need to be faithful to what is given us and to not give up hope. We must hold the vision, but we must hold it loosely, letting go of our own desired goals and leaving room. For every experience, perceived by us as good or bad, has a part in making us who we are today. This person we are today with our past experiences and our future potential becomes Holy ground for the nudges of the Spirit. Our suffering may fuel the energy and passion of the divine-led work to which we respond. God's transforming power works in mysterious and amazing ways.

These stories have taught me that one does not follow a leading alone. A divine leading implies relationship, not only with the Holy One, but with others whose lives are touched by the leading. It is vital that we encourage each other. Our leadings need to be affirmed by our Friends meetings, our churches, and our other spiritual communities. It takes a village to support a leading. On stage, as well as back stage, are a host of people offering prayers, listening, giving advice, encouraging, offering companionship, lending a helping hand, and donating money. A spouse may take on one's responsibilities, freeing that person to do God's bidding. In the drama of following a leading, many people have parts to play. Even people who seem to present some barrier, some opposition to the leading, may play a role in the divine process. None of us knows the whole picture.

The more deeply people surrender into difficult paths, the deeper grows their faith. Many of these people face difficult times and become discouraged, but they do not lose heart or give up. Some are led into voluntary poverty, wondering how they will survive. Others are very lonely, surrounded by people who have very different values than their own. I have been impressed by the willingness of these people to do what they need to do. The task may be daunting, even appearing impossible. It may take longer than we expect and happen in a way we never imagined. Yet when we place the leading as we discern it into the hands of divine providence and do everything we can do to be faithful, we can trust that whatever else is needed will be provided. Jesus taught us:

> With men this is impossible; but
> with God all things are possible.

Matthew 19:26 (KJV)

The people of these stories have, with God's help and the help of others, turned the tiny mustard seeds within their hearts into sturdy trees in the forest of life.

Bibliography

Berry, Wendell. *The Gift of the Good Land: Further Essays, Cultural and Agricultural.* San Francisco: North Point Press, 1981.

Brinton, Howard. *Friends for 300 Years.* Wallingford, PA: Pendle Hill Publications, 1997.

Cronk, Sandra. *Dark Night Journey.* Wallingford, PA: Pendle Hill Publications, 1991.

Dass, Ram and Gorman, Paul. *How Can I Help?* New York: Alfred A. Knopf, 1993.

Calvi, John. *The Dance Between Hope and Fear.* Gainsville, FL: Southeastern Yearly Meeting, 1992, 1995.

Faith and Practice of New England Yearly Meeting. Worcester: New England Yearly Meeting of Friends, 1986.

Fujii, Most Venerable Nichidatsu. *Beating Celestial Drums.* Los Angeles: Peace Press, 1982.

Havens, Teresina. *Mind What Stirs in your Heart.* Pendle Hill Pamphlet #304. Wallingford, PA: Pendle Hill Publications, 1992.

Kabat-Zinn, Jon. *Wherever You Go There You Are.* New York: Hyperion, 1994.

Kelly, Thomas. *A Testament of Devotion.* New York: Harper, 1941.

Loring, Patricia. *Spiritual Discernment:The Context and Goal of Clearness Committees.* Pendle Hill Pamphlet #305. Wallingford, PA: Pendle Hill Publications, 1992.

Macy, Joanna. *Despair and Personal Power in the Nuclear Age.* Baltimore: New Society Press, 1983.

O'Connor, Elizabeth. *Cry Pain, Cry Hope.* Waco, Texas: Word Books, 1987.

Oliver, Mary. *New and Selected Poems.* Boston: Beacon Press, 1992.

Penzer, Stella Slawin. *Bigos.* Newton, MA: Primrose Press, 2001.

Richards, M. C. *Centering: In Pottery, Poetry, and the Person.* Middletown, CT: Weslyan University Press, 1962.

Steere, Douglas, ed. *Quaker Spirituality: Selected Writings.* New York: Paulist Press, 1984.

Steere, Dorothy. *On Listening to God and to Each Other.* Philadelphia, PA: The Wider Quaker Fellowship, 1984.

Taber, Fran. *Come Aside and Rest Awhile.* Pendle Hill Pamphlet #335. Wallingford, PA: Pendle Hill Publications, 1997.

Hanh, Thich Nhat. *Living Buddha, Living Christ.* New York: Riverhead Books, 1995

Hanh, Thich Nhat. *The Miracle of Mindfulness.* Boston, MA: Beacon Press, 1987.

Walton, Marty. *The Blessed Community, the 30th Annual J. Bernard Walton Memorial Lecture.* Orlando, Florida: Southeastern Yearly Meeting, 1993.

Whitman, Walt. *Complete Poetry and Collected Prose.* New York: Literary Classics of the United States, Distributed by Viking Press, 1982.

Woolman, John. *The Journal and Major Essays of John Woolman,* edited by Phillips P. Moulton. New York: Oxford University Press, 1971.

Nudged by the Spirit

was composed on a Power Macintosh 7600 computer using Adobe Pagemake 6.5 and typefaces from the Adobe Type Library: ITC Korinna for all text plus Adobe Caslon Swash Italics and Adobe Caslon Ornaments for incidentals.

The book was printed in the United States of America by Thomson-Shore Inc., Dexter, Michigan. 60# Gladfelter Recycled paper was used for this printing of 1,500 copies.

History of the Type Faces

Korinna first appeared in 1904, introduced by the Berthold foundry into the Art Nouveau period of full-bodied proportions and unusual characater shapes. In 1974, Ed Benguiat and Vic Caruso revived Korinna for the International Typeface Corporation. It has open forms and a distinctive flavor.

Book Design by
Eva Fernandez Beehler and Rebecca Kratz Mays